Edexcel AS General Studies

Anthony Batchelor   Gareth Davies   Edward Little

STUDENT BOOK

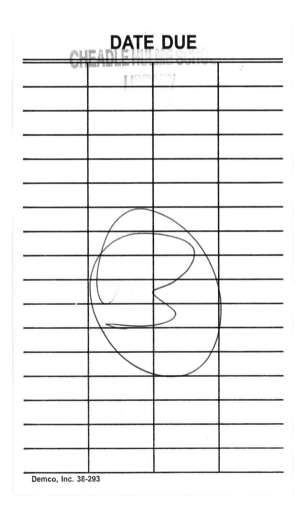
A PEARSON COMPANY

Contents

Introduction   3

Thinking and Analytical Skills   5

Unit 1 Challenges for Society

Chapter 1 What do scientists do?   9

Chapter 2 How does science affect society?   17

Chapter 3 Does science benefit society?   25

Chapter 4 What makes a humane society?   33

Chapter 5 Should the punishment fit the crime?   41

Unit 1 multiple-choice questions   49

Unit 2 The Individual in Society

Chapter 6 Is it nature or nurture that best explains society?   55

Chapter 7 Where do our values and opinions come from?   67

Chapter 8 Mass media: representation or reality?   75

Chapter 9 Do the arts challenge or reflect society?   83

Chapter 10 Is the UK really a democracy?   91

Unit 2 multiple-choice questions   101

Exam technique

Top tips   106

Answering multiple-choice questions   108

Data response questions: skills   110

Data response questions: practice   116

Extend writing questions: skills   126

Extended writing questions: practice   130

Glossary   140

Answers   157

Introduction

Why study General Studies?

General Studies is not like other subjects. As the title implies, the content covers a very broad range of topics. You need to know why these topics have been chosen and why following the course benefits you.

General Studies is designed to help you make connections between various topics and subjects and to become aware of different ways of viewing them. Since many of you follow a largely arts or science programme, General Studies offers a chance to see how issues and concerns discussed in other subjects impact on wider society, as well as on your own interests.

As it helps you gain a broader picture and to learn how to connect ideas and information from different disciplines, General Studies is a good preparation for those of you aiming for employment, where a range of problems, conflicting perspectives and other factors need to be understood, considered and reconciled. Such transferable skills will also prepare you well if you aspire to enter higher education.

General Studies should help you to ask questions and argue about issues that are important – as an individual, as a member of your family group, as a citizen of your country, and finally as a member of the human race. In order to do this you have to be able to draw upon everything you may have studied and experienced. You need to:

- have an open mind
- listen to opposing points of view
- develop arguments or points of view of your own
- weigh up the evidence
- present arguments and evidence in a convincing way to others.

Exam requirements

At AS you will take **two** papers, each of **1 hour and 30 minutes** duration. You will need to attempt **ALL** the questions. The structure of the two papers is the same:

- **Section A** has 20 multiple choice questions with 20 marks available.
- **Section B** contains one or two pieces of data on which a series of **structured questions** is based. There are 30 marks available.
- **Section C** includes two questions each linked to a piece of **stimulus material** (e.g. a table of figures, a diagram, an extract from an article). You will write a fairly short piece of extended writing on each topic. There are 40 marks available.

Key themes

The AS part of the course is based on some major themes:

Unit 1 Challenges for Society
- This unit helps you develop an understanding of some of the **problems and issues that society faces** and will face in the foreseeable future. Many issues

arise from the fast pace at which science and technology seem to develop. It helps to consider the sometimes unexpected and disturbing effects of some scientific advances. These examples may help us understand how to cope with new challenges.

- The unit also helps you to understand the **benefits that science and technology have brought us**. Do they represent successful progress? Or do we end up with different and more serious problems?
- Science and technology are not the only things that change society – **religious convictions** have always had a profound effect on the development of any society. What should be the relationship between religious belief and government?
- Finally, all societies, as far as we know, contain individuals who do not wish to conform to the norms of their society, and in extreme cases ignore the **rules and constraints** that society has developed and agreed. What should we do with such individuals?

Unit 2 The Individual in Society

- In Unit 2 the focus is on the individual. What makes us **individual**? Do we have free will? And if we are influenced, what influences us?
- Where do our **values** come from? If individual members of society now favour a multicultural and more equal society, and recognise that gender bias and ageism are wrong, what has brought about such changes?
- Although we often 'talk **equality**', why are youngsters from poor families still less likely to go to university and get a degree than those from better-off homes? Why is the life expectancy of poor people in some urban areas shorter than for better off people living in the suburbs or the countryside?
- Viewing TV is a national pastime, yet life as described in the **media** is often very different from the real world. How important is bias in some newspapers? Is the Internet a danger or an opportunity?
- How relevant are the **arts** to understanding society? Does music or contemporary writing actually influence individuals in society? How do the arts reflect the concerns and values of the artist?
- Does **democracy** really put the people in charge? Can individuals achieve changes in how political parties or government think and act? And do individuals have enough say about the part the UK plays in the world?

How to use this book

This book is designed to help you to work largely by yourself, to enable you to achieve a good grade in the AS examination. You can use it alongside a taught course as well.

The basic rule with any study is 'little and often'. You will not gain very much from ploughing through this book in a week or so. You will, however, get enormous benefit from working through two pages a week, especially if you link it to work in your other subjects and keep looking for the connections between themes and topics.

At the back of the book, there is some detailed advice for you on tackling the examination questions (pages 106–39). Practice questions with worked answers and examiner advice are provided in the style of the three sections of each paper, along with questions for you to attempt. Multiple-choice questions to test your knowledge appear at the end of each unit.

Taking it further

1. Look through the key themes for AS General Studies and then make a list of your other subjects. Link the content of these subjects to the themes in the General Studies course. For example, if you are studying history at a higher level, what major scientific and technological changes occurred in your chosen historical period(s)? Did these changes have any effect that is recognised by historians?
2. Pick a major recent news story that interests you. Look through the themes for AS General Studies and see which parts link to this story. If there is nothing else, there are likely to be issues of right and wrong, so look through the pages on moral reasoning and identify the issues that need to be resolved.

Thinking and analytical skills

Thinking through General Studies

General Studies is about the development and application of skills and techniques to issues rather than just the accumulation of knowledge. Subject knowledge is a means to an end, rather than an end in itself. General Studies uses other disciplines and provides opportunities to develop transferable skills that can benefit other areas of study.

This feature of General Studies is reflected in two key Assessment Objectives which carry 50% of the AS marks. Assessment Objective 2 requires you to:

> *Marshal evidence and draw conclusions: select, interpret, evaluate and integrate information, data, concepts and opinions.*

Assessment Objective 3 requires you to:

> *Demonstrate understanding of different types of knowledge, appreciating their strengths and limitations.*

These Assessment Objectives outline thinking and analytical skills, which are about the application of knowledge to specific issues, rather than collecting information. These skills are developed in two different ways: firstly in written material, whether essays or extended writing, and secondly in critically reading and analysing other people's work. Together they are a powerful tool which should help improve the way you accumulate knowledge and ideas and how effectively you communicate your own ideas and understanding.

Types of argument

You should know and be able to explain key terms for different types of argument; you should also be able to identify appropriate examples.

An argument is a connected series of statements designed to support, justify or provide evidence for the truth of another statement or conclusion. You need to know about five main types of argument:

- **Deductive arguments** are usually explained as *reasoning from the general to specific.* More accurately, if the premises (previous statements from which a conclusion is inferred) are true, the conclusion cannot be false. Therefore the premises guarantee the truth of the conclusion and the conclusion will not go beyond what the premises require. Deductive arguments are usually limited to inferences relating to maths and definitions or rules of formal logic. A simple mathematical example of a deductive argument is:
  Premises: *There are always three angles in a triangle.*
  The total number of degrees in the angles of a triangle is always 180.
  Two of the angles in a particular triangle add to up to 150 degrees.
  Conclusion: *Therefore the third angle must be 30 degrees.*
  The conclusion is inescapable since the premises are true. Another simple example is:
  Premises: *Birmingham is a city in the West Midlands.*
  The West Midlands is a region in England.
  Conclusion: *Therefore Birmingham is a city in England.*

- *Inductive arguments* are usually explained as *reasoning from specific observations to a broader generalisation*. The premises are deemed to provide reasons for supporting the *probable* truth of a conclusion. Different conclusions could be drawn, especially if more information was available. A simple example might be:
  For the past 50 years it has always rained in the first week of April in the Lake District.
  Therefore it will rain in the first week of April next year in the Lake District.
  The conclusion cannot be certain, but may be very likely (see also page 11).

- *Arguments from authority* are often confusing. They are not about an individual's status, reputation or position but about evidence or opinion offered by an expert on the basis of acknowledged expertise and knowledge of a relevant topic. Authority is usually regarded as a weak form of argument because two equally respected authorities may justifiably hold different and contradictory views, thus cancelling each other out. An 'authority' may not have expertise in the required area, may not be disinterested (unbiased) or may not be representative of most experts on that topic. Argument from authority is often described as a **fallacy** and must be treated cautiously.

- *Argument from analogy* is another common weak form of argument. It is reasoning based on perceived similarities between two or more things. It argues that a perceived similarity in one aspect will result in similarities in other aspects. In effect arguments from analogy claim:
  (a) is similar to (b) in certain ways.
  In a particular circumstance (a) reacted in a specific way.
  Therefore (b) should respond similarly under similar circumstances.
  The strength of reasoning from analogy depends on the validity of the similarities identified. Any conclusion can be at best only possible.

- *Causal argument* is another weak type of inductive argument. It claims that one thing happened as a direct result of something which occurred previously. Too often what we describe as causal reasoning is simply correlation. Correlation is a simple statement that:
  (a) happened first and was followed by (b).
  A causal argument must be able to demonstrate that (b) could only have happened because of the prior existence of (a). A causal argument states that:
  (b) happened as a direct consequence of (a).
  Causal arguments are complicated since few events have a single cause and coincidences happen. A strong correlation does not on its own establish cause.

Fact, opinion and belief

You should understand and be able to distinguish between knowledge, truth and belief. 'Knowledge' usually refers to information we have at our disposal. This is often described as subject knowledge. These statements all use the word 'know':

> *(1) I know Napoleon was defeated by Wellington at Waterloo.*
> *(2) I know that my Redeemer lives (Job 19:25).*
> *(3) I know you will be happy at university.*

Each statement has a similar format but means different things. Most people would accept statement (1) as factually accurate. Statements (2) and (3) are

---

Key terms

fallacy – an error in reasoning. A fallacy is different to a factual error; it is when given premises fail to provide the required level of support, although appearing to do so.

Examiners' Tips

Not every use of analogy is an argument. Analogies may simply be used to explain or illustrate meaning.

opinions: the first based on religious conviction, the second based on personal experience. 'Know' is used in different senses and has different meanings. You should distinguish between these concepts, especially if there is not an obvious difference in how ideas are expressed.

Theories of knowledge concern how knowledge is acquired and how it is classified. Key terms are fact (or **objectivity**), opinion (or **subjectivity**), knowledge, belief, moral values and truth and falsity.

- *Fact* is objective and can be confirmed and supported by evidence. It is a statement about what is 'known to be' as opposed to something that is 'thought to be'. A fact's accuracy can be established. To decide if a statement is factual you could ask:
  - Can it be established by direct observation?
  - How did the author obtain or discover these facts?
  - Is there universal agreement on the accuracy of the fact?

- *Opinion* is subjective and concerns an individual's feelings. It may be based on experience and may not have universal agreement. Opinions often contain value judgements and may not always be supported by evidence. Sometimes opinions can be verified, but often they are personal and so open to challenge. To decide if a statement is opinion you could ask:
  - Does the person use words (such as 'better', 'ugly' or 'thrilling') to interpret or describe ideas?
  - Do words suggest opinion, such as 'probably', 'usually' or 'sometimes'?
  - Could different opinions be held from the same information?

  The sky is blue is a factual statement, but *The sky is a beautiful shade of blue* is opinion. It might be generally accepted, but is open to challenge because it depends on what each person considers to be the true meaning of *beautiful*.

- *Knowledge*. Most of our factual knowledge is learnt from family or through education and experience. Much knowledge is recorded in permanent form but it is constantly increasing. Some claim that we are born possessing certain knowledge. This is called *innate knowledge*.

  Knowledge can be extended through experience or observation. Such newly discovered knowledge is sometimes called *empirical knowledge*. This discovery of knowledge is based on developing testable hypotheses by observation and experiment. More broadly it can refer to the use of experience and evidence to formulate ideas.

- *Moral values* may be treated as factual, but are really subjective. Moral values may be shared with others and help to shape behaviour. Often in speech or writing we make moral judgements. Not everybody will agree with our moral values, or with the authority on which we base them.

- *Beliefs* are things which an individual, group or society holds to be true, or acts as though it believes them to be true. They may be matters of opinion. We should be able to justify our beliefs. Equally beliefs may be matters of fact, generally agreed, and supportable with concrete evidence.

- *Truth and falsity* are more complicated. Something is true if it corresponds with the way the world is. To say something is true it is essential to show that it is consistent with available supporting evidence. A lack of evidence means the truth of a statement cannot be tested. It can only be described as false if there is evidence to disprove it. A claim is false if it does not conform to all known relevant facts. Some things (for example a child's 'imaginary friend') cannot be tested and so cannot be described as either true or false. As known facts change, earlier perceptions of truth can change. It was once believed that a flat earth (or at least saucer shaped) was the centre of the universe.

Applying analytical skills in General Studies

If you understand these terms you will adopt a more critical and analytical approach to what you write or read. Do not accept things uncritically. Analytical skills enable us to break down issues or arguments into their component parts and identify how the different parts relate to each other.

When analysing arguments, identify the conclusion and the reasons advanced for accepting it. Ask if these reasons are supported and whether the support is based on fact or opinion. Consider the type and strength of argument used. Consider different ways of thinking about an issue and examine how these relate to each other. These questions are worth asking when you evaluate any argument:

- Can the facts used be trusted? What is their source?
- Does the author have sufficient knowledge to make these particular claims?
- Does the author identify the sources used so that reliability can be checked?
- Is the evidence used relevant to the argument being presented?
- Is all relevant evidence used or has the author omitted evidence that might challenge the conclusion being presented?
- Is the evidence used sufficient to support the claim?
- Is the evidence presented primarily factual (objective) or opinion (subjective)?
- Does the author rely on emotion rather than reason and logic?
- Is the argument balanced or is it one-sided?
- Does the author show bias or consider alternative views fairly?
- Does the conclusion follow from the argument and evidence cited?

It is easy to make unsupported **assertions**. We are entitled to develop, hold and present our own ideas or opinions. We may not be challenged on our opinions, but we should be able to justify them. If our words are to influence others, they must be supported with evidence. People are more easily convinced by arguments based on fact than opinion. Opinion based on personal experience is generally more convincing than unsupported opinion.

Examiners' Tips

If asked to analyse the quality of an argument or evidence used in a passage, don't give your own opinion on the issues raised, unless you are asked for it. It is also important not simply to summarise what the author has written.

Activity

Select an opinion article from a quality newspaper on a topic you are familiar with. Use the questions (right) to analyse the conclusion, argument and evidence presented. Identify two examples of 'fact' and two of 'opinion'. Does the writer make any moral judgements? Identify two examples of the author's beliefs.

Key terms

assertion – a claim made with confidence but without any supporting evidence to justify it

Unit 1: Challenges for Society

Chapter 1   What do scientists do?

What you're going to learn:

- How scientific advances are based on induction
- How scientists propose hypotheses and test them
- How to distinguish between theories that explain the same observations
- How to recognise problems and questions that may not have scientific explanations
- How to answer 'why' questions.

Physicist Albert Einstein

Your idea of a scientist is probably based on a stereotype. You may have in mind the wild-haired and wild-eyed photograph of Albert Einstein, who is usually represented as a real brainbox.

However, it is important to realise that being scientific is a distinguishing feature of all human beings. This is clear when you come across a problem: suppose you wake up one morning and the bedroom light does not work. Depending on your level of knowledge and experience, you go through sequences of actions based on ideas about possible explanations:

Has the bulb blown? Is the switch broken? Is there a power cut? Has the fuse blown? Has the house wiring broken somehow, somewhere? Am I dreaming?

A systematic approach will resolve your problem; if it doesn't, then you call in a more knowledgeable expert. While these activities are not really 'doing science', you are behaving scientifically because, based on an observation about the universe – 'my bedroom light doesn't work' – you make some likely explanations which are possible to test. As far as we know such behaviour is typical of humans and has made us incredibly successful as a species.

You should also be clear that science is a never-ending attempt to understand the universe and how it ticks. A scientific explanation, or theory, is of use to us only if it has stood up to repeated testing by experiment. If an experiment gives results that are incompatible with the explanation, then either the experiment or the explanation (or both) need to be carefully reconsidered.

Activity

Brainstorm your idea of a scientist. List all the adjectives that come into your mind that you would associate with the word 'scientist'. Sort them under these headings:
- positive
- negative
- neutral.

The nature of scientific explanation

It takes quite a long time to appreciate fully the nature of science and how we arrive at new theories and discoveries. There is no one commonly agreed scientific method. You may have the impression that scientists work methodically, testing and trying out all possibilities. Of course this is partly true, but many scientific theories have come to the scientist almost out of the blue. It is as though all the pieces of a jigsaw suddenly fall into place, and the result often seems completely obvious. This is not just a chance event, though, because training and skills are needed to recognise the problem and make the connections. In short, insights are made by the prepared mind.

Scientific theories are the result of observations or observable events. The events may form a noticeable pattern or several possible patterns. If the thought occurs to someone that there is a possible reason for the pattern, then they may come up with a hypothesis. In an idealised investigation there is a cyclical process of observing, predicting and testing predictions, as in the following diagram:

Taking it further

Find out how the following discoveries were made:
1. the molecular structure of benzene
2. the structure of the nucleus of the atom
3. the microbial cause of some diseases.

Is there anything in common in the way in which these discoveries were made?

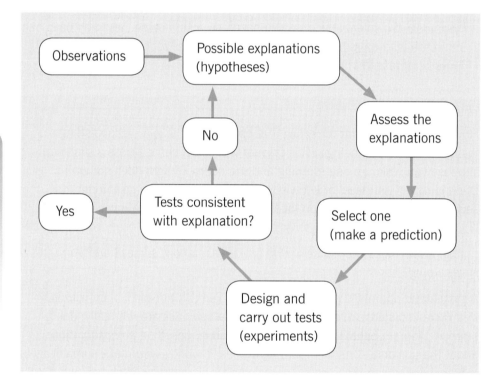

Induction and deduction

Many philosophers regard the process of forming scientific explanations as a logical process called *induction*. We owe our understanding of induction to the work of Aristotle (see page 34). Observations are used to make a generalisation or conclusion. As long as new observations are consistent with the conclusion, the conclusion is confirmed. The conclusion can only really be provisional because we cannot make all possible observations.

Compare this logic with *deduction*, which is most closely associated with mathematics. Here we work from axioms, or things that are self-evidently true. From axioms we make deductions which, if our reasoning is sound, lead to conclusions that must be true. The axioms, reasoning and conclusion is called a 'theorem'. A theorem can act as an axiom for deducing more theorems.

An example will make the processes of induction and deduction clear. Suppose explorers in a new land see a flock of birds that appear to be like crows, except that they are white. They find this surprising since all the crows they have seen in the rest of the world are black. They have been applying an inductive process in expecting that any crows in this unexplored land would be black. What conclusion can they now draw? As biologists, they would probably decide that this is a completely new species of crow. They would need to check carefully that all the other characteristics of crows – shape, size, wings, feathers, beak and claws – were within the range expected for crows. If this were so, then they would be faced with deciding if it were just a colour variety, or a new species distinct from black crows, but certainly a crow.

Another form of reasoning about the situation might go like this:

> *All crows are, by definition, black.*
> *The new birds are white.*
> *Therefore the new birds are not crows.*

The first premise sets up an axiom, the second premise is an indisputable observation, and the reasoning leading to the conclusion is inescapable. It might satisfy a logician, but the biologists will not be happy.

The (un)certainty of science

The fact that we can make observations that may conflict with a theory that has served well for a long time can make some people doubt science as a whole. Saying 'it's only a theory' suggests that what is being discussed is somehow unreliable or not to be believed; rather like equating theories with statistics in 'You can prove anything with statistics.'

However, people should realise that the certainties in life are few and far between – death and taxation are commonly believed to be the only two. (And even those, in a science fiction world, might be avoided!) The fact that scientific theories can be overturned is the great strength of science. This is why scientists must always remain sceptical and work on the basis of evidence rather than opinion or unsupported belief. The rejection or modification of a long-standing theory represents a triumph of human endeavour, not a product of weakness or uncertainty.

Activity

Debate the proposition that 'Nothing in science can be certain.'

Taking it further

What do physicists mean when they propose a 'theory of everything'?

Taking it further

1. Read up about the recent controversy about the nature of Pluto – is it a planet or not? Search term: 'Pluto not a planet'.
2. What are radio telescopes?
3. What is the Hubble telescope?
4. Planetary systems around distant stars have been discovered. Why are they of interest to us?

Success in prediction

In this section we will look at how prediction is a good indicator of the relative strength of a particular theory. We will consider examples from astronomy and medicine.

Prediction in astronomy

People have always been interested in the sky and what is in it. For example, the discovery of new planets in the solar system created much excitement in the 18th and 19th centuries.

Astronomical discoveries are almost totally dependent on having good instruments for looking at distant objects: telescopes. The first compound telescopes were made from combinations of lenses; they were used by Galileo Galilei to make significant observations on Jupiter and its moons. Isaac Newton and others developed the reflecting telescope from combinations of concave and convex mirrors, which was capable of producing much clearer images.

Key advances in astronomy:

- Kepler's laws of planetary motion
- Newton's laws of motion
- Newton's discovery of gravitational attraction.

When Isaac Newton and Johannes Kepler formulated the physical laws that define the movement of bodies and the effects of gravity, it was possible to predict the movement of planets across the sky with greater and greater accuracy. However, when more accurate calculations were made, the observed planetary movement of Uranus was found to be slightly different to the calculations. It was realised that the differences between the observations and the calculations might be due to the gravitational effects of other undiscovered planets.

This led to the identification of Neptune as planet. Galileo was the first to observe Neptune but he thought it was a fixed star because it did not appear to cross the sky in the way a planet does. So, it was not difficult to see Neptune but it took much mathematical calculation from the observed disturbance of the orbit of Uranus to work out where the disturbing planet was in the sky.

The laws of gravitation are still used to calculate successfully movements of planets and the trajectories of rockets in space missions. However, Einstein's General Theory of Relativity makes a number of predictions about gravity, space and time that are currently being tested by a spacecraft – Gravity Probe B. If the predictions are verified, it is said that there will be profound implications for our understanding of the universe.

Medical prediction

Working in a Viennese hospital for women in the 1840s, Dr Ignaz Semmelweis noticed that women giving birth in one ward were dying but others in another part of the hospital were surviving. He looked for differences in the two wards and discovered that the surviving women were treated by trainee midwives, but those in the other ward were attended by student doctors. He wondered how this might affect the health of the women giving birth and what differences there might be between the midwives and the doctors.

It occurred to Dr Semmelweis that a major difference between the student doctors and the midwives was that the former were touching corpses in their anatomy lessons. An accident that had happened to a friend of his, who cut his finger while dissecting and subsequently had a fatal infection, made him think that something in the bodies might be proving fatal. He suggested that the doctors should wash their hands after anatomy lessons. After introducing this practice the mortality rate in their ward reduced to that of the midwives' ward. So Semmelweis made a prediction from observation, then tested it; this later resulted in the theory that minute organisms could cause disease.

Falsifiability

One of the consequences of induction is that it places scientific theories in a strange philosophical position because we can never assert that a theory is, or ever will be, universally true. So how can we be confident that our theory is a good one? We can subject the theory to testing – not by trying to find another situation where we think it will be successful in providing an explanation but by deliberately trying to find circumstances where it could fail (be shown to be false), and testing it under those conditions.

This idea has been associated with the philosopher Karl Popper (1902–94). He went on further to suggest that a theory could only be considered scientific if it was open to falsification. You might ask – are there theories that *cannot* be falsified? A classic example is 'All humans are mortal.' It is impossible to test this because we have to examine every individual to make sure of his or her state of life. An opposing theory – 'All humans are immortal' – is easily falsifiable by the production of one dead person.

Simplicity is best

Scientists often have to compare theories that appear to give the same results while having different explanations. To help them do this, one self-imposed rule they use is called 'Occam's Razor'. This dates from the 14th century, when William of Occam stated that the explanation of any phenomenon should use the fewest assumptions, especially discounting those that seem to have little to do with the explanation. It is an example of parsimony, in other words, 'All other things being equal, the simplest is the best.' Popper favoured this idea as well, because the simplest explanations are the most amenable to falsification.

Activity

Find an example of the use of Occam's Razor in science.

Questions science does not try to answer

As you should know by now, science is part of human curiosity: a desire to understand what makes the world tick. However, science doesn't have the answer to everything.

'Why' questions

Kinds of questions that science cannot answer are often to do with purposes or ends. For example, many 'why' questions are not scientific, or at least you have to be careful about the nature of the 'why'.

'Why does the Sun rise in the east every morning?' can be answered by reference to knowledge of the orbit of the Earth round the Sun and the theory of gravitation. The question is, in this sense, better put as, 'What is going on that results in the Sun rising in the east every morning?' But we can challenge this by asking: 'Why does the Earth go round the Sun?' and 'Why do bodies attract one another?' The questions have to be rephrased to make scientific sense.

Another 'why' question could be 'Why are we here?' It is possible to read this question to give an answer such as, 'The reason why humans are on the Earth is that we were created here by a higher being, for purposes which we cannot understand.'

Such questions are called *teleological* questions because they ask us to believe that things happen in order that some need is fulfilled or an end or purpose is achieved. 'Why do rabbits exist?' may inspire the answer, 'Because foxes (and many other predators) need to have food.' Many people might feel very dissatisfied to receive an alternative scientific answer such as, 'Because they happen to have evolved, and, as yet, have not become extinct.' This last is not felt to give a sufficient answer, if the question was intended to be a philosophical, or possibly a religious question, rather than a scientific one.

Activity

Rewrite the following questions so that they can be considered scientific:
1. Why is grass green?
2. Why do dogs bark?
3. Why do we have to die?

Regression questions

Young children often develop the 'why' question to elaborate and (to their parents) infuriating lengths:

> *'Why did the door bang, Mum?'*
> *'Because Dad slammed it'*
> *'Why did Dad slam the door, Mum?'*
> *'Because he was cross'*
> *'Why was he cross?'*
> *'Because we had an argument'*
> *'Why did you have an argument?'*

and so on.

Such chains of questions and answers have often been used in philosophical and religious arguments, to assert or prove the existence of a prime mover, or God. The essence of this argument is that if every event is the result of an immediate cause, and the cause is a preceding event, which in turn has a preceding cause, then there must have been a first or 'prime' cause for all events in the universe.

There is not space or time here to discuss all the finer points of this regression, except to say that there is an assumption here that justification, or cause, is assumed to precede an event, in other words, the progress of time in one direction (a cause must precede an effect) is necessary for these arguments. That is not necessarily the case for all such 'why' questions.

Right or wrong?

Questions that involve moral issues and reasoning, such as 'Is this right or wrong?', are not usually decided through scientific analysis or judgement. Of course, a scientist's actions can be subjected to moral analysis. Rightness and wrongness may be considered absolute qualities by some philosophers, but relative matters by others (see page 36). Since science is concerned with the way the universe works, there can be no moral issues in the theory of gravity, or in the fact that living things die eventually.

There are also many questions that have a scientific context but which do not rely on science alone to answer:

> *'Should we stop making all nuclear weapons?'*
> *'Should we stop eating meat?'*
> *'Why don't we make everyone use renewable energy resources?'*
> *'Why don't we make everyone donate blood when they are alive and donate their organs after death?'*

Give me a definite answer!

It is dangerous to assume that there is a definite answer to everything. Scientists are not so clever that they can take uncertainty away from us. This is most apparent when we want answers from a doctor, who uses science but is often unable to soothe all fears.

For example, 'Is it *absolutely* safe to allow my baby to be vaccinated with the MMR vaccine?' The answer to this is definitely 'no' – because there are always risks associated with any medical procedure. Although the answer is no, the doctor will almost certainly advise you to have your baby vaccinated. The reason is that answers to medical questions depend on a balance of risks. The doctor's reasoning will go like this:

> *Your baby is, as far as I can tell, normal in all respects, so there is nothing specific in your baby's makeup that suggests that they will respond badly to vaccination. However, there is a tiny risk that an adverse reaction might occur (based on the statistics of all the millions of such vaccinations carried out), but that must be balanced against the very much greater risk that if your baby later catches measles, mumps or rubella, the consequences could be serious. Therefore I cannot say to you that the MMR vaccination is absolutely safe for your baby, but on the balance of risk, vaccination is a no-brainer.*

Another example of a medical query is, 'We are told that smoking cigarettes causes lung cancer. Why do people get lung cancer when they have never smoked?'

The inability to give a definite answer – yes or no – should not be held against scientists. Sometimes the answer can only based on a balance of risks; in many other cases a definite answer is not possible because the evidence is insufficient.

Activity

List the points you would use to answer one of the questions on the left. Which points are dependent on scientific evidence, and which are moral or ethical issues?

Chapter 1 Summary

By now, you should have knowledge and understanding of:

1 How scientific advances are based on induction

- Scientific explanations or theories are built up by making observations, developing a hypothesis, and testing the hypothesis.
- Induction is a form of reasoning, common in science, in which the conclusion can never be completely justified, even if the premises are true – in a sense all explanations are provisional.
- Deduction is a form of reasoning typical of mathematics in which the conclusion is always justified and inescapable, provided the premises are true. Scientists may use deductive (mathematical) reasoning as part of testing hypotheses.

2 How scientists propose hypotheses and test them

- Scientists make observations and create explanations in many different ways.
- Ideally there is a cyclical process of testing and rejecting hypotheses, until the one that explains most is selected.

3 How to distinguish between theories that explain the same observations

- Scientists test theories by trying show that a prediction from it is incorrect – this is the principle of falsifiability.
- Scientists adopt the principle of parsimony (Occam's Razor) so that if there is no other difference the explanation that is simpler, using fewer assumptions, is preferred.

4 How to recognise problems and questions that may not have scientific explanations

- Problems which pose an ethical or moral problem may not be open to scientific investigation.
- Questions which ask, 'What is the meaning of...', or which deal with purpose, may also not be open to a scientific investigation.

5 How to answer 'why' questions

- Questions are not always straightforward, even though they look very reasonable. This is particularly true of questions that begin with 'Why...?'
- A question like 'Why did X die?' can be asking, 'What was the medical reason for X's death?', which will have a scientific explanation.
- If 'Why did X die?' means, 'Is there a particular reason why X, of all people, died?', the question could be answered by religious reasoning.
- Why' questions often need to be broken down to be absolutely clear about the meanings of the words they use.
- Broadly speaking, if there is sufficient evidence, science can attempt to answer questions that begin 'How...?' as an alternative to 'Why...?'
- Many medical answers are statistical. We should make an effort to understand why this is so, and not expect impossible assurances.

Chapter 2 How does science affect society?

What you're going to learn:

- How some scientific discoveries and theories can change the way we see the world
- How these changes can alter the course of history
- How new scientific discoveries are used to create new technologies
- How the new technologies are used to solve human problems
- How the use of new technologies can bring new problems, sometimes as a direct result of solving old problems
- How governments support scientific research.

Look around you and think how different your life would be if:

- electricity had not been discovered and exploited
- gas, coal, petrol and other non-renewable energy sources had not been exploited
- food was not produced on an industrial scale.

There are still human beings on the planet whose lives are not greatly affected by these discoveries and applications, but they are few and far between. Also their lives are being changed through the carbon dioxide emitting activities of the rest of us.

It is obvious that scientific discoveries and the technologies that they help create have a profound effect on the way we live.

Piccadilly Circus, London

It is not quite so obvious that a society can have a considerable influence on the kinds of science and scientific activities that take place within it. This is often because of the moral values held by the society, for example:

- how people feel about animal experiments or cloning
- how people feel about experimenting on humans
- how people feel about the development and use of weapons
- how people feel about stem cell research.

In the past some scientific theories and the methods used by scientists were considered to be fundamentally wrong by those in power because of their religious views: think of the Church's opposition to the theory that the Earth was not at the centre of the universe. However, it is also true today that governments may use their beliefs to control and modify the findings of science: think of the evolution versus creationism controversy.

The kind of society we live in and the amount and the nature of science taking place in it are bound together inextricably.

Activity

Choose two other technological applications that affect your daily life. List the effects on your way of life if they had not been developed.

Key terms

cosmology – the scientific study of the origin of the universe, galaxies, stars and planets

astronomy – the scientific study of planets, stars, galaxies and the universe

Scientists challenge old ideas

Over the past 600 years there have been many scientific discoveries that have challenged the religious beliefs or ideas of the time. We will look at just two of them here: developments in **cosmology** and the evolutionary theories of Charles Darwin.

The solar system

Classical **astronomy** (in the West) is based on Greek and Middle Eastern developments from several thousand years ago. Commonly held beliefs were:

- the Earth is the centre of the universe
- the earthly universe has a boundary, and heaven lies beyond it.

These beliefs suited the various mythologies and religions around at the time. This is a simplification but, in essence, the medieval world at the beginning of the 16th century believed that complete explanations for the way the world appeared to be had been worked out by ancient philosophers such as Aristotle and Plato and mathematicians such as Archimedes and Euclid more than a thousand years earlier. Medieval education and thought was therefore based on learning and regurgitating the ideas of these thinkers. Arguments and debates were often about finer points of interpretation of classical scholars' work rather than seeking different and better explanations.

The way things 'seem' is not always as they 'are'. A simple illustration of this is as follows. We still talk of the Sun rising in the east and setting in the west. In between it appears that the Sun travels from the east to the west. This illusion is produced by the rotation of the Earth in relation to the Sun. Since the Earth is so big and we're standing on it we don't notice this rotation: it just seems as though the Sun travels around us. This idea of relative motion was a big step in mankind's understanding of the universe.

The Copernican revolution and its aftermath

The idea that the Sun, rather than the Earth, was the centre of the known universe was put forward by a few writers and thinkers well before the work of Nicolaus Copernicus in the mid 16th century. However, their ideas were not supported by evidence that could be generally accepted, and flew in the face of authority.

The idea at the time was that the Sun and other heavenly bodies circled round the Earth (the 'geocentric theory'). This is an easy thing to believe, if you just consider the Sun, Moon and Earth. If there were no other bodies in the sky, then the Sun and Moon circling the Earth is an entirely consistent notion, and you would not be able to prove otherwise. The existence of other things in the sky, however, changes everything.

It was an important religious concept that the Earth was the centre of the universe, presumably because God created things that way and had a special place for mankind in the scheme of things. Therefore other bodies must circle the Earth. However, there is a big problem. These bodies did not seem to go round us in a neat circular way. Tracing the path of the Sun and Moon is easy, but planets did not follow a circular path round us – they appeared to wander around (it was easy to see Mars, Venus and Jupiter with the naked eye).

This problem had been known about since classical times, and a solution of sorts was given by the Greek-Egyptian astronomer Ptolemy in the 2nd century AD. He worked out a system of epicycles whereby the planets performed loops on their circular path round the Earth. This provided reasonably good predictions of where the planets would be in time to come.

In the early 16th century Copernicus proposed a 'heliocentric theory', where the Sun was at the notional centre of the universe. His explanation provided a far more accurate and logically acceptable explanation of planetary motions. His work was further refined by Kepler (who showed that the paths of the planets around the Sun were elliptical, not circular), Galileo (who observed the moons of Jupiter, and experimented on falling bodies) and Newton (who developed the idea of gravitational attraction to provide an explanation for planetary movement).

It important to realise that these ideas had, and continue to have, practical applications. The ability to navigate and explore, the sites and orientation of buildings, agriculture and the adaptation to seasonal changes in the weather are all influenced by an understanding of the natural world. Even in weaponry, understanding the laws governing motion enabled more accurate predictions of the flight of projectiles.

Charles Darwin and evolution

Evolution and **natural selection** are ideas that were developed much later than modern forms of astronomy and cosmology, but they are just as mind-blowing in their significance for scientific thought. They also challenge people's ideas about the meaning of their own existence.

Evolution challenges some fundamental religious beliefs about how human beings came into existence, for example the Abrahamic religions (i.e. Judaism, Christianity and Islam) believe that all living things, including humans, were created by God, and that man has a special significance to God. The literal truth of the sacred writings that outline these beliefs has been followed for centuries, which is why a scientific theory that questions the creation story produced such a furore in the 19th century.

The evidence for evolution is very robust, as it is for natural selection, yet religious fundamentalists go to incredible lengths to cast doubt on it. There is no reason why any scientific theory cannot be challenged, indeed progress in science depends on such challenges, but so far, evolution has won the day.

Taking it further

In the 16th century, how did navigators and sailors know where they were on the oceans? What advances were necessary to work out a position on the Earth's surface?
Use these search terms: latitude, longitude, sextant, chronometer.

Key terms

evolution – the process of change over time in the inherited characteristics of organisms

natural selection – the process by which organisms adapt to their environment through changes in their gene make-up; according to Charles Darwin, this is the major driving force of evolution

---

Taking it further

1. Why was Darwin's idea of natural selection so controversial at the time?
2. Why does the theory of evolution still cause controversy today?
3. Why do some religious believers find it possible to accept evolution and others do not?

Use these search terms: natural selection, genetics, creationism.

New science creates new challenges

Major scientific discoveries have big knock-on effects. Although in themselves they satisfied scientists in explaining natural phenomena, the uses to which the discoveries are put usually create profound and difficult problems in ethics or have unforeseen long-term consequences. Here we will look at two examples of highly significant scientific advances: the discovery of atomic structure and gene theory.

Atomic structure

The discoveries of Marie Curie, Ernest Rutherford and Albert Einstein are very significant in this story, but their work depended on many others.

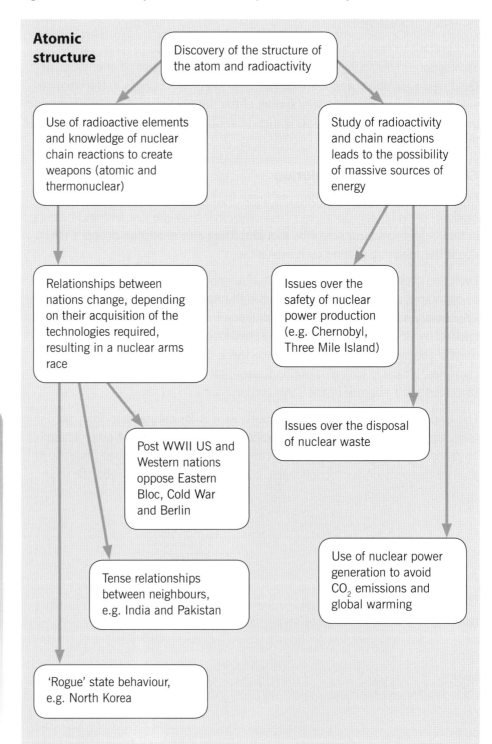

Taking it further

1. Find out the major features of the work of Marie Curie, Ernest Rutherford and Albert Einstein.
2. Find out the differences between:
   • nuclear fission and nuclear fusion
   • radiation and radioactivity
   • atomic and thermonuclear weapons.
3. List the advantages and disadvantages of nuclear power production and compare them with the use of coal, oil and gas for power production.

Gene theory

Developments in biology, biochemistry and genetics have similar knock-on effects to those in physics. For example, an understanding of genes and how they work, together with the identification of genes present in an organism, raise a host of issues in individual health and public medical provision.

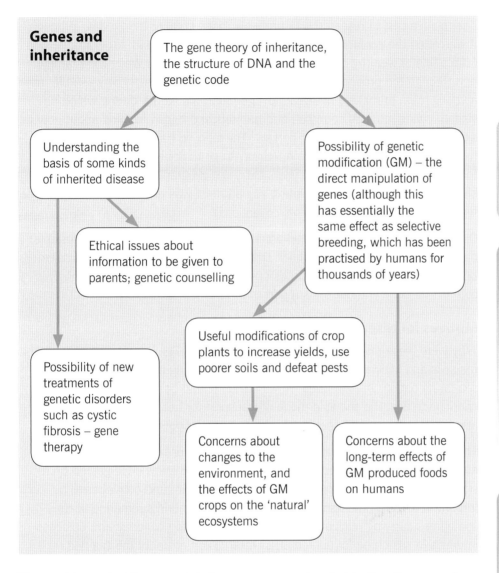

Genes and inheritance

The gene theory of inheritance, the structure of DNA and the genetic code

Understanding the basis of some kinds of inherited disease

Possibility of genetic modification (GM) – the direct manipulation of genes (although this has essentially the same effect as selective breeding, which has been practised by humans for thousands of years)

Ethical issues about information to be given to parents; genetic counselling

Useful modifications of crop plants to increase yields, use poorer soils and defeat pests

Possibility of new treatments of genetic disorders such as cystic fibrosis – gene therapy

Concerns about changes to the environment, and the effects of GM crops on the 'natural' ecosystems

Concerns about the long-term effects of GM produced foods on humans

Key terms

human genome – the full collection of genes that produces a human being

Taking it further

1. List the ethical issues involved in the development of GM crops.
2. With other students discuss the implications for society if a gene causing obesity is discovered.
3. What are the pros and cons of the genetic screening of the whole population?

Examiners' Tips

There are likely to be questions in any General Studies examination that ask you to reflect on the benefits and disadvantages of technological advances. Sometimes you will be given an example, or you may be expected to produce an example yourself. A good idea is to make sure you have prepared material on a couple of examples: they could be the two discussed here, or you could think of some others yourself. When answering a question, make up a table with benefits on one side and disadvantages/costs on the other before you try to write an extended answer.

The working out of the complete **human genome** has led to the discovery of many genes that could have implications for the health of individuals. New genes with such potential are being discovered every day. One problem is that many of these genes only indicate an increased risk of a condition such as breast cancer or prostate cancer, not a certainty that the individual will develop these diseases. Also, our knowledge and understanding of these discoveries is at an early stage.

Another complicating factor is that many businesses are developing the technology for analysing the genome from a small sample of body tissue. Some companies are offering a complete gene analysis to private individuals (genetic screening) for a price. Such companies may also develop therapies or treatments to remedy genetic problems diagnosed in this way. It is easy to see how these costly services might be developed and abused. However, this is a developing area and much research is being carried out. There are enormous benefits for national and social services if the potential for an individual to develop disease can be discovered.

How society supports scientific activity

Up to 150 years ago, scientific research was largely carried out by individuals, sometimes based in an institution such as a university. Their ability to communicate with other researchers was limited to writing letters or attending meetings.

The relative cost of research was probably much smaller than today, although it was often the preserve of wealthy people. Charles Darwin, for example, was from a line of wealthy doctors, and his wife was from the Wedgwood family, rich through the production of pottery and china. As a result, he was able, as a young man, to make a five-year voyage round the world, during which he visited a wide range of countries and habitats and began to think about how to explain the diversity of life that he saw. The ship he travelled on, HMS Beagle, had been commissioned by the Admiralty to go to South America and cross the Pacific, and during the five years carry out geographical, geological and biological studies. Darwin's position as naturalist was unpaid, and he spent the rest of his long life working on his collections.

Compare this with modern expeditions with similar objectives to inaccessible parts of the ocean in submersibles. Dozens of scientists and technicians would be involved, and millions of pounds spent on equipment and personnel. This couldn't be done without the support of government or business.

Motives for research

Why were these research programmes carried out? The importance of exploring the seas and knowing more of the coasts surrounding them is obvious to any sea-faring nation. All countries with a coastline and ports have used, and continue to use, the sea as a mode of transport for heavy goods, and, to a lesser extent these days, people. So there is an economic reason for the work.

There are also military aspects: defending a coast, or being able to approach and maybe attack an enemy, depends on maps and knowledge gained from scientific exploration. Undersea exploration has been, and continues to be, important to governments with the capacity to maintain submarine fleets, sometimes carrying nuclear weapons. There are also economic and business interests in searching for oil and other reserves on or under the sea bed.

From this we can identify possible motives for governments in carrying out or supporting expensive scientific research:

- Economic – to do with increasing the wealth of a country
- Strategic – to do with defending the nation against potential aggressors
- Militaristic – to do with threatening other countries
- Image building – to do with promoting a positive view of a country
- Co-operative – to do with sharing costs and esteem with other countries.

Particle physics

Research into particle physics is seen as investigating at the very edge of our understanding of the universe. There can be nothing more fundamental than knowing about the structure of matter, and this requires big machines that need huge quantities of energy. In essence they throw particles at one another as fast as possible and record the particles and energy that result. These experiments, based on predictions made by theoretical physicists, have produced much data. The new generation of these machines are hopefully going to answer questions raised in cosmology.

It is not possible to predict how such knowledge may affect human beings in the future. Nearly all of this research is carried out by international teams of physicists, supported by grants from governments. The results are of little immediate use to industry, although the technology involved is highly advanced and does have an economic impact.

Space exploration

Space exploration depends more on the use of advanced technology than new science, and is generally used to place scientific instruments, some of which are new, in places where they produce better results. The best known is the Hubble Space Telescope, which has produced stunning pictures of outer space.

Placing men on the Moon in the 1960s was almost certainly motivated by national rivalry between the USA and the then USSR, and has produced little that could not have been obtained by placing instruments there instead. Investigations of Mars, Jupiter and Saturn have been carried out by small space vehicles, and have discovered much of great interest about our solar system. The projects cost a great deal, and have to be planned meticulously years in advance. They tend to be financed by individual countries, because of the potential military aspects of putting devices into orbit using rocketry.

The independence of science

Science is an activity that is supposed to be free from political, social and economic pressures. Scientists are assumed to have an unwritten code of practice: they are expected to be honest when reporting their results, even if they are not what they were expecting. They benefit from the work of other scientists, so it should be in their interest to share their findings and cooperate.

However, if their research work requires funding, those providing the funds may expect scientists to produce results that benefit the organisation. Moreover, the organisation or company may feel that the work they have paid for should not be handed to rival organisations. There may be much pressure on scientists in these organisations to behave in secretive ways.

There may also be pressure on researchers to hide results that may be inconvenient for the public to know. For example, drug companies may only want to publish the results of work that show their products to be very effective, and to gloss over when there appears to be no effect. When experiments and surveys in the 1950s started to show that smoking could be linked to lung cancer and other diseases, tobacco companies sponsored research which tried to show otherwise. Worse still, it has been found that the companies also paid fees to influential individuals and journalists to distort and question the research showing the links. Of course, all results are open to challenge and confirmation, but considering the profits of the companies concerned, one can see why such practices came about. They are probably still effective even today.

Another kind of pressure on scientists is to set aside evidence that casts doubt on work that they may have spent their lives on. This is an understandable human reaction, but it is damaging to science. Sometimes the pressure on the scientist, or perhaps the desire to come first with an outstanding discovery, leads to fraud. Scientists are like the rest of us – good in parts – and a few have succumbed to the temptation to cheat.

Activity

1. Find out the cost of the new machines that research particle physics, and which countries are involved. What benefits do these countries appear to receive? (Search terms: hadron collider, Higgs boson, particle accelerator, CERN, Fermilab)
2. List reasons for and against the UK government supporting particle physics projects.

Taking it further

1. List the scientific benefits from the 1960s Moon landings.
2. Find out the likely future of the International Space Station.
3. What are the Mars Rovers? What is surprising about them?

Chapter 2 Summary

By now, you should have knowledge and understanding of:

1 How some scientific discoveries and theories can change the way we see the world

- Before the 16th century ideas about the universe had little basic theory to go on.
- Educated people were taught classical ideas.
- Overturning a classical view, for example in astronomy, resulted in a profoundly different way of looking at the world.

2 How these changes can alter the course of history

- Accepting evolution through natural selection caused arguments amongst those who believe in the literal truth of religious texts.
- It questioned ideas that, for example, humans were special creations with a unique status in the world.

3 How new scientific discoveries are used to create new technologies

- Atomic theory leads to new ways of isolating elements and creating new compounds. These lead to new materials.
- The discovery of nuclear chain reactions leads to the exploitation of atomic energy – for power production and for bomb making.
- The development of genes and theories of inheritance lead to animal and plant breeding strategies.

4 How the new technologies are used to solve human problems

- The discovery of radioactivity and an understanding of how different forms of radiation are produced lead to useful medical technologies (X-rays).
- Understanding electricity leads to new ways of power transmission, so that whole populations can have heating and lighting more easily.

5 How the use of new technologies can bring new problems, sometimes as a direct result of solving old problems

- The dangerous effects of radiation are only discovered after X-rays are widely used in medical diagnosis.
- Using coal, gas and oil as energy sources inefficiently leads to atmospheric pollution (acid rain).
- The use of fossil fuels leads to increased levels of atmospheric carbon dioxide.

6 How governments support scientific research

- Governments support scientific research for different reasons – economic, strategic, military, public relations and to encourage international cooperation.
- Industry and business support scientific research, expecting that there will be an economic benefit, or profit, from it.
- Scientists are expected to be totally honest in reporting their findings, but sometimes they are under pressure to be secretive.

Chapter 3   Does science benefit society?

What you're going to learn:

- How science and technology are related
- How science and technology benefit society by improving food supplies, medicine and using machines
- How scientific advances can create new problems
- How scientific research is supported
- How environmental problems are created and how they might be resolved
- How some groups in society oppose aspects of scientific and technological development.

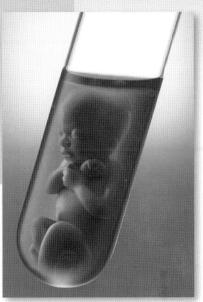

The word 'science' is a way of describing human curiosity and the desire to explain more of the world and universe in which we live. It has helped us to understand more about our bodies and our minds, and how we come to be.

Science benefits society mainly through activities that we now class as technology, where discoveries are applied to problems. Scientific research is intended to explain the world better, but most scientists also assume that their work will provide human benefits, or ease problems. Most people involved in science believe that better explanations will ultimately provide better outcomes for humankind.

A major benefit of science is the production of cheaper and more widely available solutions to human problems. For example, better understanding of the causes of disease, which in turn depends on greater understanding of how the body works, can lead to improvements in the human condition.

Science and technology have enabled the human population to increase rapidly, particularly in the last 150 years, through improvements in medicine, food production and the use of machines. The effect of this human increase is to put stress on the environment in which we live and potentially make irreversible changes, which in turn might make it impossible for humans to survive. Increased use of technology has potentially damaging environmental effects. So benefits come with hidden costs.

At the moment, humans generally seem to believe that the changes we have brought about can be countered by the application of yet more technological development. For example, if we can't get enough oil to make petrol, then we should make petrol from a renewable source, biofuel, which only requires plant material that we can grow. The disadvantage of this is that the land needed to grow enough plants to make biofuel has to be taken away from the land we need to grow food crops. It is more than likely that a huge change in our lifestyles, and in the size of the human population, will be needed to ensure the future of humankind.

Activity

Who first used the phrase 'knowledge is power'? List reasons why such an idea is important.

Science is supported in many ways

Scientific research

Science is promoted universally. It is an essential part of the curriculum in nearly all educational systems and a core faculty in most universities. Society clearly values science if it uses so much resource in training young people. This is an example of 'enlightened self-interest' on the part of governments: money spent on training will be earned back by economic growth. Developing countries almost always look to acquiring modern technology and scientists as a key to a more hopeful future.

Since the 1960s in the UK, and in response to the spiralling costs of scientific research, government support has taken an increasingly hard line: in order to get central government funding, research has to show that it produces real and immediate financial benefits. The problems that a proposed programme of research sets out to solve must meet criteria to show that the funding is going towards an appropriate and useful purpose and not some obscure field of study that appears to have no economic benefit. This approach is entirely understandable and is used to gather political support.

Large industries also see the point of research that can lead to business improvement. Since the 19th century, large industrial companies have made fortunes through their own research sections, or by sponsoring university research. Good examples are the huge chemical industry in Germany, the petrochemical industry in the USA, the development of petrol engines and, in the late 20th century, the pharmaceutical industries.

One problem with supporting only research that is directed to economic or business benefit is the question of cutting-edge research into new areas where there may not appear to be positive economic outcomes. No business is likely on its own to support research into fundamental particle physics for two reasons – the economic benefits are not obvious enough in the short term, and the cost is extremely high. So governments support such programmes through grants, ultimately from taxation, and in some cases as part of an international programme to share the costs. Governments want to support such research for several reasons, including desire for esteem, national pride, as well as the hope that a breakthrough brings more distant unsuspected benefits – in the case of particle physics, new forms of energy resources.

Medical research, too, is expensive. Pharmaceutical companies spend enormous sums on developing and, more importantly, testing new drugs. For these companies, costs have to be recovered in sales, usually to national health services. The costs of production have to be recouped by the business, and since many drugs are specific to particular diseases or conditions that have relatively few sufferers, they will remain expensive. Research into drugs is also a secretive affair and companies are very wary of revealing details of their research, for fear of their competitors, until they acquire suitable patents and protection. This is a tragedy for science, which depends on sharing information about ideas and developments.

Charitable support for research

Much medical research is supported by charities devoted to sufferers from specific problems – cancer, kidney disease, strokes, Alzheimer's disease and many others. The amount of money given by millions of donors is stupendous;

for example, Cancer Research UK raised £411 million in 2006/7 – well over £1 million per day. The money supports over 4000 researchers and hundreds of drug trials. There are several advantages to this form of support:

- Donors can be recruited from people who have been touched by cancer in some way – nearly one in three of us will have cancer at some time in our lives, and everyone knows a cancer sufferer, or is related to one.
- Money donated is given favourable tax status: the government allows donations to be free of income tax and will refund to the charity any tax that has already been paid.
- The work of the charity does not have to satisfy the need for profit for shareholders; therefore more of the donated money goes to research.

A scientific advantage of this form of support is that research can be directed towards problems that are 'cutting edge' but which might not provide sufficient immediate profit to a commercial business. So, for example, discovering the way in which genes control the activities of the cell, or how genes can be switched on and off, is critical to understanding bigger general problems of biology, as well as understanding how a cell becomes cancerous.

Individuals or companies who have made large profits and have become very wealthy sometimes start their own charitable foundations, or make huge donations to existing charities. The charity also benefits from the relief from taxes. Charitable giving is called philanthropy (from the Greek word meaning 'love of humanity').

Environmental research

Here there is more reason for countries to combine their resources – the weather doesn't respect national borders. The Intergovernmental Panel on Climate Change (IPCC) was established in 1988, under the leadership of the UN. It does not carry out research itself: its job is to assess and bring together any research on the environment, climate and weather systems that throw any light on climate change. By drawing together and evaluating the worth of all this research, it has provided the stimulus for further research, and has alerted governments to future concerns.

Communications and development

One of the more attractive aspects of humanity is the way in which responses to tragedy and misfortune seem to happen almost spontaneously. Major environmental disasters, such as earthquakes, floods and hurricanes, produce reactions from all over the world. This is no doubt due to the rapidity and graphic capability of modern communications, so that when disaster strikes, the results are flashed around the world in minutes. The same communication systems can bring about the rapid responses needed to provide food, shelter and general relief.

The information technology revolution has helped the technological development of countries that did not benefit from the prolonged industrial revolution in Western countries or from the enormous natural oil resources of the Middle East. Countries such as India, with large populations, are seeking to maximise their skills in these technologies since the initial outlay is much less than developing conventional engineering.

Taking it further

With other students, find out the current situation with global warming – what temperature rise is predicted and within what time? What is the variation in estimates? Then review the actions that we can take, either to reduce the effect of global warming or to alleviate its consequences.

Technology creates new problems when solving old ones

Mankind's use of technology is a double-edged sword. The roaring success of humanity in terms of successful colonisation of almost every corner of the planet in the last few thousand years is mainly through the development of problem-solving behaviour. Many other animals, particularly our nearest relatives, can solve problems, but the human capacity for holding problems in the mind, and working cooperatively with systems for storing, sharing and passing on information, is unique.

In prehistory we developed better systems for hunting: different weapons (which encouraged us to experiment with different materials), companion animals (which led to selecting animals with specialised characteristics) and group behaviour (creating the need for sophisticated leadership systems). Subsequently, we developed agriculture: selecting crop plants; using animals for physically demanding work such as ploughing; and inventing tools for clearing and construction. Our success has probably led us to believe that all problems can be solved. Not everyone believes this, of course, but humans in view of their history are encouraged to be upbeat and positive about their own capability.

If science is an expression of the curiosity to know more about everything, technology is our response to human need, taking from science the power to meet that need. It is also an expression of **utilitarianism**. You could say that science knows no limits, beyond the power of imaginative reasoning, but technology is tied by:

- our scientific understanding (can it be tackled with the knowledge we have?)
- the level of need (how many people does it affect?)
- the resources required (how much will it cost?)
- political expediency (do people in power perceive the need?)

In chapter 2 you can see how scientific revolutions and discoveries have knock-on effects on society. It is clear that solving one problem, or meeting one need, creates another problem and more potential needs. The massive challenge of climate change must surely make us realise that technology is not the only way that we respond to what we still refer cheerfully to as 'progress'. Collective understanding of what change and progress bring about is almost certainly essential to our future survival.

Key terms

utilitarianism – the philosophical doctrine that judges activities according to whether they promote the 'greatest good for the greatest number', i.e. whether they make more people happier

Climate change

There are opposing views, but the general consensus is that the world is warming up, mostly through human activity. On the whole this has been through the use of technology associated with energy production (power generation through the combustion of fuels) and the burning of forests in many parts of the world to provide land for crops (even though this is a very inefficient form of agriculture). What shall we do about it? How should we decide what to do?

It is our confident expectation that science will make discoveries, which can then be applied through technological skills. What might these discoveries be? Some can be predicted:

- carbon dioxide capture systems
- replacement of systems which generate carbon dioxide (designing new fuels, exploiting renewable energy)
- finding ways of reducing the amount of thermal energy arriving on the Earth
- finding different ways of moving people about
- improved communication methods so that most people don't need to move about at all
- more ways of producing food in difficult environments.

Whether these will be sufficient, and whether there will be totally novel ideas, time alone will tell.

Medicine and health

We often talk about 'battling' with serious diseases. This is more than a metaphor, since maintaining a healthy body is an ongoing fight against organisms that are trying to survive and multiply at our expense. As far as we can see this will continue for the foreseeable future, but all medical advances we have so far made have become less effective in time.

A good example is the development of MRSA. This refers to a bacterium (*Staphylococcus aureus* or SA), which normally causes no problems by living on our skin and mucous membranes. It can, however, cause serious infections if the patient is already suffering from another complaint. The development of antibiotics, for example penicillin, allowed doctors to treat these infections successfully in the past. *Staphylococcus aureus*, like most other bacteria, is no slouch because in time it becomes resistant to antibiotics, especially if it is exposed to them continually. This has lead to methicillin-resistant SA (MRSA).

The reason it has done so is natural selection: the process by which we believe living organisms have developed into millions of species in the 3.5 billion years life has existed on earth. We see this in many other situations where we have to challenge a biological problem. Another example is the build up of DDT resistance in mosquitoes carrying malaria and other insect transmitted diseases, when DDT has been over-used as an insecticide.

These examples tell us that no matter what we do on this Earth other organisms will be affected, and that they will adapt to the changes we bring about, creating new situations and problems for us to solve. This is a fundamental fact that we must learn to live with; it is worth remembering that we have also evolved, and possibly will continue to evolve in the future, assuming, of course, that we do not become extinct.

Activity

Climate change is not the only effect of human activity on the planet. Pollution from mining and escape of poisonous chemicals are also down to humans. Research an example of pollution and list the problems and outcomes of the incident.

Science, politics and religion

Scientific activities rely on a sceptical attitude. All scientific theories are open to scrutiny, to experimental testing, and rejection if they are found to lack adequate predictive power (see pages 12–13). A scientist's job is to question any belief in their area, or to apply the theories to new situations. If a belief cannot be tested (see page 13) then it is no longer part of science – for example, the existence of a soul, life after death or indeed anything labelled 'supernatural'. Such beliefs are not necessarily to be rejected; they are at the moment simply beyond the possibility of testing. If and when ways of testing are devised, then the beliefs may turn into scientific theories – which will be rigorously tested again.

Religion, on the other hand, requires belief that has to be taken on trust.

Religious objections to medical procedures

Some religions maintain strict rules in relation to the treatment of disease. Jehovah's Witnesses, for example, will not allow the use of blood transfusion, even if the sufferer's life is threatened by death. Their reasoning is based on interpretation of parts of the Old and New Testaments, from which they derive the belief that the 'consumption' of blood by any means is not allowed. They believe also that this prohibition is supported by evidence from the rise of the AIDS epidemic. Another example is that of Christian Science, whose followers believe that faith alone is necessary to cure disease, and who will only receive treatment from healers from their own church. Faith healing is sometimes based on the idea that God has punished the sinner by giving them the illness, and renewing the faith is the only cure. Bans against vaccination are common amongst other sects.

Medical procedures where there is a conflict between the duty of doctors and the beliefs of individuals – operations, transfusions and the use of drugs – are relatively easy to sort out. An adult individual has the right to refuse all treatment, and medical authorities accept this. However, religious attitudes can create conflict with social and humanitarian views. For example, where it is clear that a young child may need a blood transfusion to save its life, but the parents exercise their right for it not to be treated, social services can face some difficult decisions. If medical opinion is clear that the transfusion is essential and likely to be successful, doctors are required by their professional beliefs to do all that they can for the child and social services may step in to act *in loco parentis* (literally, 'in place of the parent'). There is a clash between a minority religious belief and the duties of medical and social workers.

Religion and reproductive biology

Things are rather different when the problem is related to medical matters such as contraception, abortion and fertility. Many of these problems are not caused by disease; they are to do with making choices about the use of the body. There may be a disease involved – most obviously sexually transmitted – but this may not be the main focus of the moral problem.

Contraception is a topic about which some religions hold strong views. For example, some Christian traditions hold that conception is a divine gift and that to interfere with it is an offence against God.

Arguments on abortion are clearly moral debates and centre on how you define when a 'person' as a unique living individual comes to be. In some beliefs, a new individual is formed at the time of fertilisation (conception), and the sanctity of this new individual must be preserved at all cost. In other beliefs a new individual is formed at birth, and therefore the embryo and unborn baby are part of the mother, thus removing or treating them is only like an operation on the mother and does not breach the sanctity of embryonic life. Depending on definitions of person and individuality, moral positions will differ, and possibly will bring about controversy for years to come. The morality may be old, but has to respond to the challenge of new discoveries of science.

Along with cloning, stem cell research has created divisions between religious believers, doctors, politicians and the general public. When a fertilised egg develops, at a very early stage the cells are undifferentiated – capable of forming cells of many different kinds. Some cells retain this ability for some time; these are called stem cells. Cells that have become changed to carry out particular jobs are said to be differentiated. Differentiated cells are not usually able to change back to divide and produce different kinds of cells.

There are two basic types of stem cell: embryonic stem cells and adult stem cells. The latter are found in parts of the adult body where new cells are needed continually, such as the bone marrow (to form blood) and the skin. The hope is that stem cells can be used to repair damaged areas, for example parts of the brain in Alzheimer's disease or following a stroke, or heart muscle after a heart attack. Stem cells are potentially very useful because they can avoid problems caused by an immune response. Adult stem cells from one person will not induce an immune response in that person but may do so in someone else. Embryonic stem cells have not yet acquired immunity and therefore it may be possible to use them in anyone, so they may be more useful.

The moral issues mostly centre on how the stem cells are obtained. Embryonic stem cells obviously can only be obtained from embryos, but in doing so the embryo may become damaged, or at least should not be allowed to continue to grow into a new individual because of the risk of damage. This means that embryos from which embryo cells are taken will be discarded. For some religious groups this represents killing an individual, and for this reason research on embryonic stem cells is controversial. In some countries attempts have been made to ban the use of them.

Activity

Minority groups exist to protest against many aspects of technological development, for example new road schemes, airport extensions, animal experiments, GM foods. Select one, not necessarily from this list, and list the objectives of the group. Identify the ethical issues raised by the objectives, and try to contrast the opposing views.

Chapter 3 Summary

By now, you should have knowledge and understanding of:

1 How science and technology are related

- Science is only limited by human curiosity and scientific discoveries are not necessarily of benefit to humans.
- Technology is the application of scientific discoveries to problems and human needs.

2 How science and technology benefit society

- Technology is as old as humans, and the development of tools and agriculture are defining points in human evolution.
- Improvements in agriculture, medicine and machines that help in physical work are continually being made.

3 How scientific advances can create new problems

- The ability to ensure human survival, through increasing food supplies and health, has led to an explosion of the population in the last 200 years, which is predicted to continue.
- Increasing population leads to pressure on the environment through destruction of natural habitats, pollution and climate change.
- Medical advances which deal with organisms causing disease have to be made all the time, because the disease organisms can themselves adapt to change.
- Almost every technological development has a downside.

4 How scientific research is supported

- Governments believe that scientific research and the technological developments that follow from it will be of economic benefit.
- Businesses and industries are competitive and new science leads to new business opportunities.
- Science is also supported through altruistic activities such as charitable giving.

5 How environmental problems are created and may be resolved

- The major environmental problem facing humanity is now believed to be climate change.
- There is much evidence that climate change is of human origin, through increasing emissions of carbon dioxide.
- Carbon emissions may only be reduced by radical changes in the way we use energy.

6 How some groups in society oppose aspects of scientific and technological development

- Since technology meets human needs, there are always going to be ethical considerations about applying technological solutions.
- Some religions have special views on the integrity of the human body.
- There are strong beliefs held about the nature of human individuality (such as when an individual acquires their identity), so that the destruction of human embryos at various stages is forbidden.

Chapter 4 What makes a humane society?

What you're going to learn:

- How societies are governed using unwritten principles as well as written constitutions
- How religion is used to establish the ethical principles on which many societies are based
- How the relationships between individuals in a society have been argued about by philosophers and religious leaders for thousands of years
- How different ethical systems can be established in secular societies
- How ethical principles governing the treatment of animals are different in different societies.

'The care of human life and happiness, and not their destruction, is the first and only legitimate object of good government.'
THOMAS JEFFERSON, President of the USA, to the Republican Citizens of Washington County, Maryland, 31 March 1809

The Constitution of the United States of America is one of the most quoted documents in the world about liberty and citizen's rights. It states the purposes of government: to create a structure to enable the different states in America to work towards common ideals and yet maintain a local government structure. It also indicates how individuals and those elected to govern them should behave to one another.

It is only one example of a constitution, but it illustrates how modern societies have tried to lay down expectations that citizens might have of their government, and vice versa, what a government expects of its citizens. We have had many forms of government in human history, all of which are concerned with the exercise of power.

Monarchies have been managed by individuals whose right to govern has either been inherited ('the divine right of kings') or seized by force. Sometimes monarchs are believed to be representatives of God, or they may actually be regarded as gods themselves.

Taking it further

1. List the most significant features of the American Constitution.
2. How did the Constitution deal with the issue of slavery, since several states allowed slaves to be owned by citizens?

How religious beliefs affect modern societies

Historically, the moral basis of society – deciding what is right or wrong – has come from religious beliefs. For example, ways of behaving may be determined by the words or writings of a prophet or holy person. These are assumed to be the directions of God. They may direct followers to behave in particular ways in order to secure their own salvation, if the religion is one that predicts an afterlife, or an ascent to heaven. Other religions may require believers to behave in ways that increase their own and others' happiness.

Greek philosophers

Ancient Greek philosophers, who lived and taught in Greece from the 6th century BC, have had a profound influence on Western thought, and it is quite remarkable that the concepts and issues that they recognised and defined so long ago remain hot issues for discussion today. Greek philosophers were held in esteem by the Christian churches in their early days.

The key figures are Socrates, Plato and Aristotle. Socrates thought that it was possible to understand the truth about such things as justice through a process of questioning, especially of people who were thought to be wiser or more experienced. Unfortunately, his enemies accused him of corrupting Athenian youth and not believing in the gods of the city, and he was condemned to death. Plato developed Socrates' work further, while one of Aristotle's ideas was that **philosophy** was a way of discovering how the world works, i.e. science as we know it today.

Secular government

The existence of different religions in one country always has the potential for conflict. Of particular concern in the UK have been protracted conflict and disagreements between followers of the Roman Catholic and Protestant varieties of Christianity in Northern Ireland. In many countries religious minorities, for example the Jews, have suffered persecution and worse. The UK has a church that is recognised by the state, and bishops of that church have guaranteed places in the House of Lords, which to many people seems out of date.

Most countries contain populations that have different religious beliefs. Since religions, by their nature, require believers to follow specific beliefs that may be completely different to other religions, it is difficult to see how a religion can occupy the governing position in a country without causing difficulties for followers of other religions (or those with no religious belief at all). For this reason, many countries, through their constitutions, make an effort to separate religious beliefs and the operations of the state. These forms of government are called 'secular'. Some states do govern on the basis of a particular religion, while tolerating the existence of other religions, but there are obvious pitfalls and dangers in this situation.

Taking it further

1. How far did the Greek philosophers affect the beliefs of the Christian church? Use these search terms: Greek Christian philosophy.
2. Did the Greek philosophers have any effect on the development of Islamic philosophy? Use these search terms: Greek Islamic philosophy.

Key terms

philosophy – intellectual enquiry concerned with questions of ethics (how one should live), metaphysics (what sorts of things exist), epistemology (what counts as genuine knowledge) and logic (what are the correct principles of reasoning)

Activity

1. The UK is said to have a *constitutional monarchy*. What are the main features of the British constitution?
2. What modern country has an *absolute monarchy*?
3. Make sure you understand the meaning, and can give one example each, of a *dictatorship*, a *democracy*, and a *republic*.
4. Names have been given to many other forms of government. Find out about two of these.

Conflict between religions and politics

The move to have a completely secular government is particularly strong in some countries, not least because those people without religious beliefs are opposed to a system of law based on beliefs some of which they cannot possibly agree with. Also, the human rights movement strongly advocates equal treatment of citizens (in all aspects of society, including the law) irrespective of their personal religious beliefs. This can cause conflict between religious leaders and politicians.

For example, in early 2008 there was controversy caused by the Church of England, when the head of the church appeared to approve the use of Islamic law (Sharia) in parts of the UK. Sharia is a legal system that regulates many aspects of life, such as diet, marriage, divorce, finance, customs and rituals, and dress. The resolution of disputes, and the handing out of penalties, is also laid down in Sharia. The controversy arose because it appeared that Sharia might overrule English civil and criminal laws, which outraged many members of the public. This, however, was not what was intended.

Another country where Sharia is resolutely contested is Turkey, where the predominant religion is Islam. Turkey adopted a secular government in the 1920s and its laws prevent the wearing of religious dress in public institutions such as schools and universities. It has taken an uncompromising attitude towards the use of Sharia, even though many Turks would accept it. The European Court of Human Rights has ruled that Sharia is incompatible with European ideas of democracy and human rights, not least because Sharia has different rules for men and for women.

Other controversies have arisen in countries with large Christian communities. The USA, whose Pledge of Allegiance was amended in the 1950s to read 'one nation under God', has a secular constitution with strict rules excluding religion from public affairs, especially schooling. However, there are large politically and economically powerful Christian groups who hold strong views on the literal truth of the Bible, who have tried to prevent the teaching of some fundamental aspects of biology in schools – notably the age of the Earth, the evolution of humans and the Darwinian theory of natural selection. So far their efforts have been successfully resisted, as have their attempts to claim 'equal time' for teachers to present fundamentalist Christian beliefs on these subjects. It is unlikely that they will stop trying, however, and it is said to be unthinkable that a presidential candidate in America would admit to not believing in God.

Taking it further

1. Different religions have very different beliefs. For more on these visit the BBC website www.bbc.co.uk/religion/religions
2. Does atheism qualify as a religion?

Activity

1. Other countries where religions, politics and government are in conflict are Tibet, Nepal and several Middle Eastern countries. How are these conflicts being resolved?
2. Discuss with other students whether there will always be such conflicts.

Examiners' Tips

When answering any essay or short question that involves different beliefs, it is important that you consider beliefs other than your own. If you restrict your answer to a description of your own beliefs, you will restrict the marks you will be able to receive. This is because the specification expects you to look at two or more sides of an issue. You are at liberty to come to a conclusion which coincides with your beliefs, but you must consider alternatives.

Human rights and responsibilities

You need to have some understanding of the different ways we can decide whether something is right or wrong, or in other words: what are our ethical principles or moral values? There are, of course, many different views. For some religious believers, their moral beliefs come from holy books or statements of their prophets. There is no simple way of resolving different views on moral values – they have occupied philosophers for thousands of years, so we have not room here to consider all their ideas. For the purpose of this summary, we will try to present some basic moral arguments.

Rules of nature

Some believe that ethical principles come from basic rules of nature; they are in a sense objective, and not determined by our personal, subjective viewpoint. According to this view, we have no choice in deciding what is right or wrong: we just have to learn the rules.

For example, we would probably agree that we have a duty as parents to look after our children, or that we should not kill other humans. We are bound by these duties; moral arguments that use a sense of obligation or duty are called *deontological* (from the Greek word *deon* meaning duty). Rights arise because you expect other people to have a duty towards you – you have a right not to be hurt by someone else, and they have a duty not to hurt you. If you have carried out work for someone, you have a right to payment for that work, and they have a duty to pay you.

This point of view was elaborated by John Locke in the 17th century, who suggested that the laws of nature demand that you should not harm anyone else's life, health, liberty or possessions. From this Thomas Jefferson derived the US Declaration of Independence – that human beings have the rights of life, liberty and happiness. Governments do not create moral rights: as stated in the US Declaration of Independence, they are universal and they are equal (the same irrespective of gender or race).

Moral relativism

A different approach is to say that all moral values are determined by human invention. This is called *moral relativism*. Each individual alone may determine his or her moral standards, or alternatively they are imposed by the culture in which one lives. Moral values therefore can be quite different in different societies and at different times.

We might say that we can only decide on the moral worth of an action by looking at the outcomes. This is called *consequentialism*. One important form of it is known as *utilitarianism*: the consequences of an action should produce pleasure or happiness, or reduce pain or unhappiness, and this should be so for everyone. There are different forms of utilitarianism, but you should be most concerned with the rule-based utilitarianism of John Stuart Mill. For example, look at theft – clearly something that most people think is morally wrong. Utilitarians would judge that theft is morally wrong because the consequences of theft are bad for everyone. Therefore a rule against theft is morally binding (it has utility) because adopting it means that the outcomes are favourable for everyone.

Yet another way of deciding on moral rules is by accepting that humans have the free will to do anything to anybody. If that is so, then all humans would be better off if they decided that their society had moral rules than if it did not. Without rules, we are all at the mercy of others acting in their own self-interest. Thus it is in our own interests mutually to agree to rules defining a civilised society, such as on theft, lying and killing. This is known as the *social contract*. The best-known proponent of this view is Jean-Jacques Rousseau (1712–78).

All of these moral systems depend on different views of human nature. One of the basic assumptions of modern societies is that all members must be treated equally. Sometimes this is confused with saying that all humans are equal (meaning 'the same'). They do not appear to be so, physically or mentally. Equal treatment probably explains why international bodies have produced principles or declarations, which they expect all countries to follow. Two of the best known are those of the UN and the EU.

United Nations Universal Declaration of Human Rights

In December 1948, the newly formed United Nations adopted a Declaration of Human Rights to which all members of the UN would adhere. It was largely the outcome of the terrible events leading up to and during the Second World War. The Declaration consists of 30 Articles. For example, Article 1 states:

All human beings are born free and equal in dignity and rights. They are endowed with reason and conscience and should act towards one another in a spirit of brotherhood.

Article 4 states:

No one shall be held in slavery or servitude; slavery and the slave trade shall be prohibited in all their forms.

Very few would disagree with such powerful intentions. However, some of the Articles have been criticised. There is fierce debate about the nature and meaning of economic rights, and Article 25 on rights to health care raises issues about how such rights can be funded. Some Islamic states believe that the Declaration is too heavily weighted towards secular beliefs, and have prepared versions that take more account of their religious positions.

European Convention on Human Rights

Adopted by the Council of Europe in 1950, the European Convention on Human Rights consists of 18 Articles designed to protect human rights and freedoms, many of which are very similar to those of the UN Declaration. In addition, the convention set up the European Court of Human Rights, to which individuals can appeal if they do not achieve satisfaction in their national courts.

Activity

With another student, choose two Articles from the UN Declaration of Human Rights and discuss why they have been included.

Taking it further

Find out how Islamic organisations have accepted, modified or questioned the UN Declaration of Human Rights.

The relationships between humans and animals

The relationship between humans and the natural world, especially animals, is complicated. Biologists accept the evidence that humans evolved from nonhuman primates and they have described the physical changes that took place during this evolution – in the skeleton, brain and posture. From the evidence of tools, buildings and archaeology there are clear changes in behaviour and social relationships over thousands of years. In the development of agriculture and the domestication of plants and animals, humans have used the natural world to improve their lives. No other animal has successfully exploited so many other organisms for its own purposes.

The human use of animals

Domestication has usually involved selective breeding so that organisms with traits that can be used for our benefit are chosen and those less useful are discarded. Virtually all animals and plants used by humans have a long history of artificial selection.

Animals may be used:

- as food: they can be milked, hunted or farmed
- to help us hunt (as companions or transport)
- to carry out useful work – hauling, pumping, transporting
- for communication
- to provide useful materials (for example, hair, fur, clothing)
- to act as companions or pets
- as sources of entertainment
- as surrogates for humans in the testing of foods, cosmetic and medicines
- scientifically to discover more about the workings of living things
- more recently, to supply animal organs for transplantation.

Ethical concerns

Concern about human rights has a long history. The idea that animals may have rights is a more recent development, and there is much confusion and much emotional discussion about the ethics of our relationships with animals.

Look at this issue from both extremes:

> **Humans** *have to feed, should not starve; should be able to reproduce and maintain their population.*
> **Animals** *have to feed, should not starve; should be able to reproduce and maintain their population.*

In either case, what is most important is survival for any animal, indeed for any organism. If we regard humans as another animal, albeit with a rather successful evolutionary history, whose activities affect the environment of the whole planet, then we might argue that the same ethical rules apply to animals including humans. In which case, to ensure survival, any animal has a right to live, and this might involve eating other animals. Some animals, carnivores, are adapted to eat only other animals. But what about a prey animal's right not to be eaten, and having a right to life?

If we regard humans as somehow different ethically from other animals, and it is difficult not to do so, then, because we are capable of predicting results of actions, the ethical principles by which humans decide their actions are different to those that might be thought to apply to other animals. From this it can be argued that humans, partly because the increase in their numbers has had such a devastating effect on the planet, but also because they are aware of the results of their own actions and have choices, have a special relationship with the rest of the living world. Most of us would agree that humans have some kind of duty of care towards other living things.

You will find, when you look at other people's views and their reasons, that there is a range of ideas on these matters. You may think that moral philosophers and religious thinkers should be able to lead us through these problem situations, but they too come up with conflicting points of view.

We can try to work things out scientifically. Biologists view all living things as having basic common characteristics, i.e. possessing some kind of nucleic acid and being able to multiply. Biologists might say that maltreating a plant in a pot by allowing it to dry out is the same ethically as failing to give a caged laboratory rat water, because both are living organisms. However, most people would say that the plant is incapable of feeling pain in the same way as an animal (as far as we know, and others might disagree). Consequently legislation in relation to animal welfare is based on the pain that is suffered by an animal.

There is an artificial distinction between pain as suffered by vertebrates compared with that experienced by invertebrates. However many fishermen are convinced that vertebrate fish that are hooked by the mouth, unhooked and thrown back do not feel pain. Pain is partly subjective and we don't know how other people and animals experience it, although recent research on the brain and nervous system is telling us more.

Animal welfare and animal rights

There are many animal welfare groups and organisations, such as the RSPCA and PDSA in the UK, whose objectives are to reduce the pain and suffering caused to animals, both domestic and agricultural. They do not campaign for animal rights, only for humane treatment. There are strict laws governing animal welfare in the UK, but none of them acknowledges animal rights as a legal issue.

Animal rights groups (sometimes referred to as animal liberationists) have a different objective. With varying degrees of commitment to the actions they are prepared to carry out, they promote the idea that animals have rights of a similar nature, and in some cases identical, to human rights.

Taking it further

Work out some of the moral arguments in making the following decisions:
1. Choosing to wear a fur coat that belonged to a grandparent.
2. Volunteering to take part in tests of a new drug.
3. Smuggling a much-loved family pet into a country that bans animal imports.
Hint – in moral decisions it is not only your own position that you need to consider, but also the effects of your decisions on others.

Activity

Look at this list of human actions :
1. keeping a dog as a family pet
2. keeping a guard dog
3. keeping a dog to search for avalanche victims
4. keeping a flowering plant in a pot
5. keeping cut flowers in a vase
6. keeping a cow to obtain milk
7. keeping a bull to provide meat
8. killing aphids that are infecting your roses
9. testing a new shampoo on a rabbit's ears, without damaging the rabbit
10. hunting a fox
11. shooting an elephant that was threatening to destroy your home
12. using a vermicide (chemical) to remove parasitic worms from your cat

With a friend or friends, work out what moral values and reasoning are involved in each case. Decide whether these actions are right or wrong. Which moral system have you used to make your decisions?

Examiners' Tips

If you are asked a question on this topic in a General Studies examination, you should not fall into the trap of answering only from the perspective of your own beliefs and emotions. To gain good marks for these questions, you must look objectively at whatever evidence is presented, or at the possibility of your own bias affecting your answers. That is not to say that you must reject your beliefs, only examine them alongside others.

Chapter 4 Summary

By now, you should have knowledge and understanding of:

1 How societies are governed using unwritten principles as well as written constitutions

- There are many different forms of government, some based on the same principles as others, others very different.
- The USA has a written constitution, based on the idea of natural law, where citizens have basic rights and expectations.
- The UK has a constitutional monarchy, without a written constitution, and laws that are partly determined by precedent.

2 How religion is used to establish the ethical principles on which many societies are based

- Ethics is the branch of philosophy which deals with right and wrong, and the principles we can use to decide our moral values.
- A religion is a set of beliefs that is established by considering human relationships with the supernatural or a creator.
- These beliefs often define the nature of right and wrong using rules given by prophets of the religion.

3 How the relationships between individuals in a society have been argued about by philosophers and religious leaders for thousands of years

- Ethical systems do not have to rely on religious beliefs to support them.
- Most societies contain communities which have different religious beliefs.
- In societies where one religious belief is dominant, groups with different beliefs may suffer discrimination.

4 How different ethical systems can be established in secular societies

- Solving the problem of co-existence of different religious beliefs in one society often depends on the acceptance of a secular government.
- In these societies, individuals often have rights that enable them to have considerable freedom.
- International bodies such as the United Nations and the European Union have established codified systems of rights.

5 How ethical principles governing the treatment of animals are different in different societies

- The use of other living things for human purposes has a history as old as civilisation.
- In the past the treatment of animals has not been greatly considered.
- A moral approach to animal welfare has come to be a part of what makes up a humane society.
- Laws and regulations governing the care of animals have been developed in many countries.
- Some believe that animals have rights which are equivalent to human rights, and campaign to legislate for these.

Chapter 5 Should the punishment fit the crime?

What you're going to learn:

- The relationship between laws and civil liberties
- Different types of crime
- The causes of crime
- What punishment is intended to achieve.

Read any newspaper or watch the news and you will understand the significance of crime. Whether in the news or as entertainment, crime seems to be a part of everyday life. It is interesting to consider how attitudes to crime have changed over time and between societies. It has been estimated that the 18th century saw more crimes added to the laws of England and Wales than at any other time in our history. By 1820 there were over 200 crimes, mainly against property, that could be punished with the death penalty, besides less serious crimes that were met with less severe penalties. In several countries today public execution is still used, as is mutilation for crimes such as minor theft.

Daniel Defoe in the pillory, London, 1702

Crime affects us all, both directly and indirectly. The chances of any individual being a victim of crime are relatively small, but we all have to pay the costs of crime through our taxes and through the effects that crime has on society and social values. There are probably very few people who will be able to go through life without breaking any laws, but most of us are not natural criminals. Given a free choice we would probably all choose to live in a peaceful and crime free environment. However, this is not possible.

Crime only occurs because there are laws to define what society considers acceptable behaviour. The Bible claims, 'Where there is no law there is no disobeying of the law' (Romans 4:15). Imagine what life would be like if there were no laws and everybody was free to do exactly what they wanted without regard for the interests and needs of others. Life would become impossible. Laws are created by society for the protection of the values of society and the defence of the rights of the individual. We should recognise that laws can only work effectively if they have the consent and support of the population. Sanctions, or punishments, exist to underpin the operation of the law for the good of all. In a democracy we have an established system for changing and improving laws.

Activity

In the 18th and early 19th centuries punishment of criminals was a public spectacle. Discuss why punishment is no longer 'seen to be done' in most countries. Is this an advantage or disadvantage for a modern society?

Activity

In groups list the rules of the institution you attend. Use the headings 'formal' and 'informal'. Who made these rules and how (effectively) are they enforced? In what ways do they make the institution a better/worse place for individuals?

Key terms

rule – a regulation or principle governing conduct or procedure within a given sphere

law – a rule or set of rules regulating the activities of members of a country or community and enforced through penalties; something regarded as having binding force

rule of law – the restriction of power by well-defined and established laws

The relationship between law and civil liberties

All institutions, from families upwards, have **rules**. These may be informal and just understood, or formal and written down. Sometimes sanctions are enforced if rules are broken. Little children may suffer punishment on the 'naughty chair' or, when older, be 'grounded' after failing to behave according to a desired pattern. We all make our own rules, and they work as long as people understand them and accept them. If rules are ignored they must be enforced or changed. Sanctions available in families are often quite limited, varying from family to family. Schools and workplaces have more formal rules with specified sanctions.

The rule of law

It is often claimed that we live 'under the **rule of law**'. This means that everyone is subject to the **law** and must obey it or suffer sanctions. Laws are simply rules that are designed to control the behaviour of individuals and groups towards each other and towards the state. There are major differences between laws and the rules that families or institutions have. Laws:

- are binding on all members of society: no one is above or beyond the law
- are usually written down
- have often been developed over a long period of time
- have associated enforceable sanctions for breaches of them.

In the UK there are different types of laws, which can be made in several different ways:

- laws approved by parliament (statutes)
- European laws, which can take precedence over UK laws
- common law has developed over hundreds of years and is based on custom or judicial precedent (i.e. court decisions made previously when judges have tried a similar crime); this is sometimes referred to as 'case law'
- delegated legislation, whereby approved institutions or government bodies are allowed to issue regulations to clarify or extend statutes (laws).

Each type of law can be enforced through law courts or appropriate tribunals and carries specified sanctions. In the UK there are two forms of law: criminal and civil. Breaches of criminal law can lead to fines or imprisonment and are investigated by the police. Civil law is when an individual takes action through the courts to determine responsibilities or to seek damages.

Respecting the law

In theory most of us accept that society needs laws if it is to function effectively. However, it is easy to act as though laws only apply to other people. Think of the number of car drivers regularly exceeding speed limits, even though they know the slogan 'Kill your speed or kill a child'. Think of the number of drivers using mobile phones while driving. Consider those people who take small items from work without permission. In theory we accept the need for laws when they affect other people or protect our personal interests, but many of us seem content to assume that otherwise perfectly good laws don't apply to us.

Any laws restrict our freedom to act as we choose. Most of us will happily accept laws about violent behaviour, which could inflict physical or mental harm. We are happy to have a police force dedicated to protecting society against violent and anti-social individuals and equally enthusiastic about laws that protect our property. However, we are generally less enthusiastic about laws that appear to restrict our own individual freedom of action.

'Liberty', or the National Council for Civil Liberties, is a non-party organisation dedicated since 1934 to campaigning against laws that they feel infringe fundamental rights and freedoms. Issues on which Liberty has campaigned recently have included torture; anti-terrorism laws; privacy; rights of asylum seekers; equality; freedom of speech; human rights; and the rights of young people.

These issues can divide society and also lead to conflicting reactions. For example, most people are concerned by night time disturbances on urban streets, but at the same time are uncomfortable with the restrictions of ASBOs (anti-social behaviour orders) or the use of mosquito repellers (low level sonic devices that only affect young people) to disperse groups.

The effects of crime

Crime affects everybody. Obviously victims, whether of crime against property or against the person, suffer most, but in addition to short-term loss or suffering there are long-term effects that are difficult to quantify. People affected by crime can include:

- victims' families
- housing estates targeted by burglary, drug-dealing, gangs
- late night travellers on public transport
- the elderly who feel vulnerable (especially to anti-social behaviour and violence)
- the families of criminals who suffer the effects of fines or imprisonment
- society as a whole.

Everybody in society is a victim when crime is committed. Society must pay the final cost, whether of compensation to victims, punishment of offenders or increasing spending on police forces. Perhaps the main costs are damage to social values and attitudes.

There are several indicators of our concern with crime. Walk down any street in any town and you will see burglar alarms on many houses, or hear car alarms. Go through any city centre and your actions will be recorded by hundreds of CCTV cameras. Drive down any main road and you will see large numbers of speed cameras (also called safety cameras or traffic enforcement cameras). It has been claimed that we are living in a 'Big Brother' surveillance society, in which our every move is monitored and recorded. A key debate is about how we achieve a balance between limitations on the freedom of the individual and protection of the individual against the actions of criminals.

Taking it further

Choose any one of the issues on which Liberty has campaigned recently. Research the steps taken by Liberty to bring about a change in the law or to prevent new laws being passed by parliament. To what extent do you feel Liberty is justified in these actions?

Activity

Discuss whether there are circumstances when the government might be justified in using dispersal orders or restrictions on movements. When are restrictions not justified?

Activity

Should we give as much attention to victims as to offenders? Discuss whether victims should be allowed to address the court before a criminal is sentenced.

Examiners' Tips

The issue of balance between restriction and freedom is emotive, especially to those involved with the law. It is important when writing on this topic that you recognise the strengths as well as the shortcomings of each viewpoint.

Different types of crime and their causes

Crime is an umbrella term covering a range of activities of different types and severity. One feature that all crimes share is that they concern actions that result in a breach of the law. Murder and terrorism are extreme, while other crimes may seem relatively trivial, but all such activities are classified as crimes. Subdividing categories of crime helps us to understand them. The government distinguishes between *summary* and *indictable* offences. Summary offences, such as motoring offences or minor theft, are dealt with in a magistrate's court. Indictable offences are more serious and carry heavier penalties; they are tried in crown courts before a jury. Indictable offences include:

- theft and handling stolen goods
- criminal damage
- burglary
- violence against the person
- fraud and forgery
- drugs-related offences
- robbery
- sexual offences.

Each of these offences can be subdivided. For example, 'violence against the person' includes:

Minor violence	Serious violence
less serious wounding	homicide
threat or conspiracy to murder	attempted murder
common assault (no injury)	child destruction
harassment	causing death by dangerous driving
possession of weapons	serious wounding
cruelty or neglect of children	other acts endangering life

Another classification of crime is by type: crimes against property; crimes against the person; and crimes against the state. It is easy to overlook two significant forms of crime. 'Victimless crimes' are where no individual directly suffers harm of a physical or financial nature. Such crimes include adultery, other consensual sex crimes, bigamy, blasphemy, electoral fraud, black market trade and trespass. Some question whether these really are crimes, saying we should be free to act as we wish provided no one is harmed (libertarianism). An alternative view is that public interest (or society) suffers and must be protected as much as individuals. 'White collar crime' is another often overlooked form of crime. This is crime committed in the work-place by high-status people. Sometimes described as middle-class crime, it includes infringement of patents and copyright; misrepresentation; fraud; bribery; insider trading; computer crime; and forgery. Though costing millions of pounds a year, it rarely results in criminal action.

What causes crime?

This question has concerned social scientists and official bodies for many years. There are many possible answers, including:

- *Physiology*: some theories suggest that certain people may be predisposed to crime for genetic reasons. Such theories are rarely held today, but it is believed that some people may commit crime because of bodily chemical imbalances, poor diet or, more frequently, through the influence of or need to fund drug and alcohol habits.

Activity

Use the Internet to investigate and list the official Ministry of Justice subdivisions of some of these indictable offences. What *tariffs* (the Ministry of Justice's recommended term of imprisonment) are laid down for each offence? Compare and comment on your findings.

Activity

Use a variety of newspapers to identify reports of different types of crime. Which types of crime are most frequently reported? What language is used to describe each type of crime? Consider the appropriateness of the punishments awarded.

- **Psychology**: some theories claim that upbringing (nurture) in either criminal or deprived homes may encourage criminal behaviour, or that criminal behaviour may result from (often temporary) mental illness.

- **Society**: some explanations blame society and the social structure. They suggest that poverty or material deprivation, poor education standards or limited employment opportunities may drive people into a life of crime to compensate for their deprivation. The media are accused of encouraging crime by portraying and glamorising it. Newspapers are accused of encouraging crime by creating moral panics (see page 77).

- **Peer group pressure**: this theory suggests that young criminals are initially influenced by the behaviour, expectations and values of their older associates. A similar idea is that youths growing up in 'criminal' areas will be socialised into accepting criminal behaviour patterns.

Crime does not have a single cause but results from a combination of factors. However, in the 1990s the sociologist Charles Murray has argued that economic and social conditions have created an underclass in the UK and USA linked to trends in unemployment and crime.

How much crime is there?

Media reports often imply that crime is a constant occurrence, directly affecting everyone and threatening social collapse. This contrasts with evidence from the Ministry of Justice and official crime statistics. What is the true picture?

Available evidence is contradictory. Official statistics give details of recorded serious crime, but are often regarded as unreliable since they depend on crimes that have been reported and how the police record them. Crime figures point to trends over time, but it is queried whether such trends reflect what is happening or simply mirror police and government priorities.

British Crime Surveys (BCS), regular surveys of victims of crime carried out for the Ministry of Justice, are often regarded as more accurate than police figures. BCS suggest only half of all crimes are reported, often because victims see them as trivial or unlikely to be dealt with effectively by the police. BCS surveys give a better indication of trends because they retain a consistent terminology and methodology. They suggest that there is a substantial 'dark figure' of crime. The dark figure refers to crime that has occurred but which is not officially known to the police and so does not appear in police statistics.

A concern often raised by the media is that crime is increasing and threatening social stability. They regularly question what can be done to reduce crime and deter criminals. The law supposedly is a deterrent, but it is impossible to say what crimes have not been committed because of this deterrent effect. However, fear of being caught seems to be a better deterrent than conscience.

Detection rates vary between types of crime and geographical areas. This may be because of government priorities and the differing attitudes of police forces. Generally speaking crimes of violence, especially murder, are more likely to be solved than theft or car related crimes. Criminals committing crimes with low detection and punishment rates are less likely to be deterred than those committing crimes where the police are more successful.

Examiners' Tips

In any exam you may get questions that test use and application of number. Statistics are an excellent source for such questions. Use official statistics to practise your numerical skills, especially in terms of simple calculations; percentages; mean, mode and median; and the interpretation of graphs and tables.

Taking it further

Compare local crime figures for a five-year period as reported in BCS and police statistics. What trends are revealed? What are the main similarities and differences between the two sets of figures? Compare your own findings with how the local media (newspapers or television) report on crime.

Activity

Use the Justice Ministry website to research crime detection rates in your own locality. Identify any trends and discuss whether these rates would (a) encourage or (b) discourage local residents concerned with perceived increases in criminal behaviour.

What is punishment intended to achieve?

Different forms of punishment have been used through the ages by different societies and in response to changes in social attitudes and circumstances. Many UK laws were originally based on Christian principles. One of the earliest meanings of punishment used in the Bible was compensation, as illustrated in the teaching 'an eye for an eye and a tooth for a tooth' (Exodus 21:24). Compensation was also a key feature of Anglo-Saxon laws. Aethelbert of Kent, perhaps Britain's first Christian king, issued a law code in about AD 600 which starts: 'One who steals the property of God and the church shall pay twelve-fold compensation.' The rest of the code defined different rates of compensation for different offences.

Types of punishment

Today our laws and ideas about the purpose of punishment have changed. We have developed a range of punishments appropriate to different offences and offenders, including:

- *Fines* – financial punishments imposed for relatively minor offences or as the settlement of a claim. They may be used either in place of or alongside community service orders. Larger fines may be given independently or alongside shorter prison sentences. They are said to be a cost-efficient and fair form of punishment for non-violent offenders.

- *Community service* – used instead of a prison sentence or a fine. Community service orders involve a fixed number of supervised hours of specified work. They may be linked to the type of offence that is being punished and should not be confused with voluntary community service.

- *Custodial sentences* – normally referred to as imprisonment. This punishment is used particularly for violent crimes, persistent offenders and those considered as being a threat to society. It is an expensive form of punishment and the current prison over-crowding crisis has encouraged the use of alternatives. In some countries costs of prison are reduced by imprisoning offenders only at weekends and allowing them to return home to work on weekdays. Their earnings are used to pay compensation to victims.

- *Probation* – the suspension of a jail sentence. A convicted criminal believed likely to respond positively to probation is returned to the community but must abide by conditions laid down by the court under the supervision of a probation officer.

- *Electronic tagging* – a form of surveillance where an electronic global positioning system (GPS) device is placed on an offender as an alternative to prison under conditions set by the courts.

- *ASBOs and ABCs* – comparatively recent developments designed to put a stop to **anti-social behaviour** rather than to punish offenders. The ASBO is statutory, and carries legal force; the ABC is an informal procedure which offers greater flexibility. Because it is formal, the ASBO is easier to enforce.

Capital punishment (execution or the death penalty) and corporal punishment (physical punishment such as beating or mutilation) are no longer legal in the UK but are still used in a few countries.

Key terms

anti-social behaviour – behaviour which causes or is likely to cause harassment, alarm or distress to one or more people who are not in the same household as the perpetrator

ABC – an informal Acceptable Behaviour Contract

Taking it further

Whenever a dreadful murder occurs, newspapers carry demands to restore the death penalty. Research and discuss or debate arguments for and against the reintroduction of capital and/or corporal punishment in the UK.

What is the purpose of punishment?

There are many different views about what punishment should achieve:

- *Retribution (or revenge)* – punishment for its own sake, based on the principle that offenders should suffer for what they have done. It is an expression of society's moral objection to crime and the behaviour of the criminal and is a reaffirmation of the values of society. People who favour retribution often argue in support of **exemplary sentences**.

- *Incapacitation* – designed to make it impossible for criminals to offend. Usually this refers to imprisonment, but in some countries it may describe corporal punishment in the sense of amputation. It was also used in the past when criminals were either exiled or transported to distant lands. There has been discussion of using chemicals or surgery to change the nature and personality of offenders. The main purpose of incapacitation is to protect society by removing from offenders the opportunities to commit crime.

- *Reformation or rehabilitation* – to change the behaviour of an offender so that they live according to mainstream values. It is often suggested that education and humane conditions are the best way to achieve rehabilitation. Since the 1991 Criminal Justice Act the attitude of both main political parties has been towards harsher and more severe penalties, with greater emphasis being placed on retribution rather than reformation.

- *Reparation* – the idea that offenders should compensate victims for the suffering they have caused, either financially or by doing work for them. It is believed that this could help reform offenders by making them face the results of their actions.

Does punishment work?

Many people ask whether prison as a punishment is really effective. It has been called a university of crime: there are strong arguments that suggest that many new offenders are turned into experienced criminals there. Some argue that other forms of punishment are more effective, especially with young offenders. Others claim that conditions in prison should be made worse so that prisoners learn their lesson through suffering. There is a high rate of re-offending amongst former prisoners.

The government claims that crime is declining, although it accepts there has been an increase in certain types of crime. In 2006 a Home Office report claimed a 42% reduction in the amount of crime since 1995. It argued that increased resources for the police and a more stringent sentencing policy have acted as an effective deterrent to criminals. It also suggested that as individuals we are less likely to be victims of crime today than at any time in the previous decade. However, the prison population is greater now than at any time in the past, as is the rate of re-offending and reconviction amongst adults.

Who are the criminals?

Crime is not the preserve of any one socio-economic group. Conviction records suggest that the more traditional 'blue collar' crimes are usually committed by working-class males. Fraud and forgery are usually committed by members of higher socio-economic groups with responsible positions in employment.

Key terms

exemplary sentence – a punishment more severe than might normally be expected, intended as a warning to other potential criminals

Activity

Discuss whether conditions in modern prisons are too comfortable. Who suffers most as a result of imprisonment – the criminals or their families?

Activity

Discuss whether punishment is successful in reducing crime and criminal behaviour. What criteria should be used to judge how 'successful' punishment is?

Taking it further

Investigate the socio-economic background of perpetrators of a specific crime, such as burglary, and its geographical distribution. Which socio-economic groups are the most likely targets for burglars? Explain your findings.

3. The experiment has been carried out probably because

   ☒ **A** there are concerns about the effect of mobile phone radiation on the body

   ☒ **B** the researchers want to find out more about skin proteins

   ☒ **C** it is believed that too many people spend a long time on their mobile phones

   ☒ **D** health and safety is very important in Finland

(Total 1 mark)

Answer ALL the following questions.

4. The difference between scientists and technologists is

   ☒ **A** scientists invent new devices, technologists build them

   ☒ **B** scientists build new devices, technologists invent them

   ☒ **C** scientists make discoveries, technologists make useful things

   ☒ **D** scientists make useful things, technologists make discoveries

(Total 1 mark)

5. Jumping into a fast flowing river to rescue a drowning person is an example of

   ☒ **A** altruism

   ☒ **B** egotism

   ☒ **C** humanism

   ☒ **D** idealism

(Total 1 mark)

6. The positions of stars in the night sky were very important in the 16th century to

   ☒ **A** priests

   ☒ **B** doctors

   ☒ **C** farmers

   ☒ **D** sailors

(Total 1 mark)

7. Natural selection was an important scientific theory in the 19th century because

   ☒ **A** it helped animal breeders to produce healthier animals

   ☒ **B** it made Charles Darwin famous

   ☒ **C** it destroyed religious belief

   ☒ **D** it explained the great variety of life on earth

(Total 1 mark)

8. 'You shall not kill' is an example of

    ☒ **A** consequentialism

    ☒ **B** natural law

    ☒ **C** social contract

    ☒ **D** socialism

    (Total 1 mark)

9. Producing biofuels to replace petrol and diesel fuels is **not** good for the environment because

    ☒ **A** to make biofuel uses too much energy

    ☒ **B** to make biofuel we have to clear lots of forest

    ☒ **C** biofuels produce more carbon dioxide

    ☒ **D** biofuels use up too much oxygen

    (Total 1 mark)

10. Analysis of the human genome is a benefit to the individual because

    ☒ **A** it helps you predict the sex of your children

    ☒ **B** it tells you if you are suffering from cancer

    ☒ **C** it warns you of possible health problems

    ☒ **D** it predicts how long you will live

    (Total 1 mark)

11. Space exploration is useful to society because

    ☒ **A** it makes money for research

    ☒ **B** it prevents a country from attack

    ☒ **C** it provides useful technological spin-offs

    ☒ **D** it makes people feel good

    (Total 1 mark)

12. The ruler of a country is a military officer who has complete power over the armed forces and civilians. The government is said to be

    ☒ **A** an absolute monarchy

    ☒ **B** a constitutional monarchy

    ☒ **C** a dictatorship

    ☒ **D** a republic

    (Total 1 mark)

13. Ethics is a branch of philosophy which helps us

☒ **A** to decide what is right or wrong

☒ **B** to decide what is beautiful

☒ **C** to reason correctly

☒ **D** to tell the difference between fact and opinion

(Total 1 mark)

14. Smoking bans in public places have been introduced in order to

☒ **A** protect the rights of smokers

☒ **B** discourage smokers from smoking

☒ **C** make places healthier to work in

☒ **D** take away the rights of smokers

(Total 1 mark)

15. Induction is a form of reasoning in which

☒ **A** facts are used to make generalisations

☒ **B** a hypothesis is used to make observations

☒ **C** rules are used to decide on actions

☒ **D** the conclusion is always true

(Total 1 mark)

16. 'We have eyes in order that we can see' is an example of

☒ **A** causation

☒ **B** teleology

☒ **C** deduction

☒ **D** coincidence

(Total 1 mark)

17. Which of these gives information about crime from a victim's viewpoint?

☒ **A** the British Crime Survey

☒ **B** police recorded crime figures

☒ **C** recorded crimes by type of offence

☒ **D** types of crime based on age and sex

(Total 1 mark)

18. Look at this table giving details of males aged 21 or over found guilty of offences by type of sentence, 2002, and answer the questions which follow.

	As a percentage of number of people sentenced				All sentenced	
	Absolute or conditional discharge	Fine	All community penalties	Immediate custodial sentence	(=100%) (numbers)	Rates per 100,000 aged 21 or over
England	7	73	12	9	927,810	51
Wales	6	75	11	7	59,291	59
Scotland	8	68	10	14	75,564	43
Northern Ireland	4	71	16	9	17,537	31

Adapted from *Regional Trends* 38

(a) The total number of offenders who received penalties other than fines in 2002 were

☒ **A** 108,020

☒ **B** 228,031

☒ **C** 237,644

☒ **D** 305,157

(b) The term 'custodial sentence' means that offenders are

☒ **A** fined

☒ **B** imprisoned

☒ **C** made to wear an electronic tag

☒ **D** put on probation

(Total 2 marks)

19. A summary court is presided over by

☒ **A** a barrister

☒ **B** a jury

☒ **C** a magistrate

☒ **D** a police officer

(Total 1 mark)

20. Which of the following crimes is best described as a 'white collar crime'?

☒ **A** burglary

☒ **B** criminal damage

☒ **C** drug dealing

☒ **D** fraud

(Total 1 mark)

21. Read the following passage and answer the questions that follow.

> Historically most societies used forms of capital punishment as a method of dealing with criminals and political opponents. Today most societies have discontinued its use, although some, including the USA, India and Japan, still use it. China executes more people each year than any other country. In 2006 there were 1591 confirmed cases of execution worldwide, of which over 1000 took place in China. Another term for capital punishment is the death penalty. It is a very contentious issue. Those who support capital punishment argue it is a deterrent, prevents repeat offending and is an appropriate punishment for murder. Opponents of the death penalty argue that it can lead to the irreversible punishment of innocent people, discriminates against the poor and minorities and does not deter criminals any more than life imprisonment. Above all they claim it has a corrupting effect on the values of any society. It is illegal according to the European Declaration of Human Rights.

(a) Is the statement 'Capital punishment is an appropriate punishment for murder'

⊠ **A** belief

⊠ **B** fact

⊠ **C** fact and opinion

⊠ **D** fallacy

(b) Which of the following statements is supported by evidence in the passage?

⊠ **A** Only India, Japan and the USA still use capital punishment

⊠ **B** Capital punishment is only used to punish murderers

⊠ **C** More criminals are executed in China than in any other country

⊠ **D** Any EU country can use capital punishment if it wishes to

(Total 2 marks)

22. A secular form of government is one in which

⊠ **A** all rules are based on a holy book like the Bible

⊠ **B** the government is elected every seven years

⊠ **C** everybody is expected to follow the same religion

⊠ **D** religious belief and the operation of the state are separate

(Total 1 mark)

Unit 2: The Individual in Society

Chapter 6   Is it nature or nurture that best explains society?

What you're going to learn:

- How far genetic factors influence behaviour and life chances
- How social factors dictate life changes and social mobility
- Ways in which society has changed; more equal, more multicultural
- How and why family life has changed
- The impact of having a welfare state for 50 years and the importance of human rights
- The significance of massive changes to work, transport and communication.

BROKEN FAMILIES MAKE SOCIETY UNSTABLE

Are youngsters nowadays just bad or badly brought up? Society 'works' when people know how they should behave and treat others. If a mum or dad isn't at home to teach them, what chance have they got?

This chapter discusses key ideas such as social mobility and life chances; so you must learn about the importance of family, school, education, communication and work in shaping our individual attitudes, values, aspirations and achievements. You must also understand how certain changes – for example, in transport and communication – have made society in the early 21st century almost unrecognisable in some ways compared to the 1950s and 1960s. This chapter is about understanding THEN and how we got to NOW.

Activity

Look at this picture of schoolchildren in the classroom in the 1960s. How does the picture look different from a photo of schoolchildren which could be taken now? What changes have occurred?

Genetic factors influencing behaviour and life chances

While the links between DNA, gender, genes and physical traits are now largely taken for granted, there is much debate about the whole question of genetic determinism: mutations of single genes can make someone susceptible to hereditary diseases such as cystic fibrosis and sickle cell anemia, while Down's syndrome is thought to arise from the abnormal duplication of a chromosome. Genetic determinism also embraces the belief of many neuropsychologists that mental illnesses can be predetermined by genes and are therefore unavoidable. In logic, if a person's behaviour is determined by genetic influence, they cannot be blamed for any wrongdoing which results.

If we have free will and our biology does not influence or affect our behaviour, then we need to consider how environment impacts on behaviour, life chances and even life expectancy. If we watch lots of violent videos or if we mix with violent people, does this make us more likely to become murderers ourselves? Could the environments in which we live affect the development of particular sexual inclinations or the likelihood that we might wish to express ourselves artistically in particular ways? Social determinism looks at interpersonal relationships to decide whether or not they might lead a person to behave in particular ways. For example, if a student only attended single-sex schools, would it have any impact on their behaviour as an adult?

The debate about the importance of 'nature' (our genes) as opposed to 'nurture' (the environment) has been conducted for years. The question is whether our genes are responsible for everything about us: not just our physical characteristics, such as eye or hair colour or the existence of freckles or a particular blood type, but also our psychological traits such as intelligence, personality or temperament – perhaps a disposition to sing or fight or be artistic or athletic. Some people suggest there are genes which control sexual orientation or fertility, while others think that those traits may be as much to do with the environment (e.g. family, school, locality, peer groups, media images and other influences) as with our genetic make-up.

It is obvious that physical characteristics are mainly hereditary – how often do you hear relatives comment that a young person looks just like an aunt or grandparent or other member of the family at a particular age? However, debates continue over whether more abstract traits such as intelligence, personality, aggression and sexual orientation are also determined by an individual's DNA. Investigations often focus on twins (identical or non-identical) or siblings (brought up together or separately) when contrasted with fostered children with no blood relationship. Often siblings who have been separated for almost a lifetime are found to like the same music or food and have the same interests (for example, gardening or studying birds) or behaviours (they may speak or hold a telephone or cut a cake in distinctive, recognisable and almost identical ways).

If it was only environment that mattered then any two children brought up under the same conditions would turn out very similar, regardless of differences in genes; yet studies from families, boarding schools and children's homes have demonstrated that this doesn't happen. However, to emphasise the importance of our genes (and perhaps the lesser importance of environment), studies of identical twins do show that they often closely resemble each other, whether brought up together or not. So many biologists conclude that genes alone cannot determine a trait because genes cannot be taken in isolation. DNA engages in complex ways with messages from other genes and signals from the environment.

It seems that at the level of individuals, certain genes influence the development of a trait within particular environments. So measurements of how much a trait is influenced by 'nature' versus 'nurture' will depend on the particular environment and genes examined. Writers such as Richard Dawkins assert the importance of genes in determining adult behaviour.

- Often genes may contribute psychological traits such as intelligence and personality and be inherited from one parent or generation to the next.
- In very few cases is it fair to say that a trait is due almost entirely to nature, or almost entirely to nurture. But most diseases now strictly identified as genetic have an almost 100% link between having a special gene and the disease and a similar correlation for not having either (e.g. Huntington's disease).
- Alternatively, such traits as the specific language we speak are entirely environmentally determined.

But the significance of the environment is emphasised by sociologists who point out that 'nurture' can sometimes have a massive impact compared to 'nature'. For example:

- in cities such as Sheffield or Birmingham people in richer areas may have a life expectancy of ten or more years longer than those who live in poorer areas;
- bright five and six year olds from poorer homes might be overtaken educationally by less able youngsters from richer homes within just 12 or 18 months of having started school.

Others, such as Matt Ridley (author of *Nature via Nurture*), argue that it is our environment that affects the way our genes express themselves. In reality, in most cases both 'nature' and 'nurture' play a key part in explaining such features as ageing, personality and behaviour.

Taking it further

Manipulating genes is questioned by some on ethical grounds. Debate these questions with other members of your class:
1. Is it wrong in principle?
2. Do parents have the right to use such technologies to make 'designer babies' or to influence a child's characteristics (e.g. height or hair colour), perhaps to improve life chances?
3. Would intervention in a person's genetic make-up be justified if they had some abnormality?
4. Are we in danger of creating 'Frankenstein people'?

Social factors influencing behaviour and life chances 1

Individuals' 'life chances' are the opportunities each person has to improve their quality of life. Originally proposed by the sociologist Max Weber, the concept covers social factors such as how education, health, material reward and status mobility impact on individuals and families.

When we discuss 'life chances' we are thinking about how equal different people are in our society. Although living standards have improved for most individuals in recent generations, the gap between rich and poor has not been eliminated; so inequalities persist and the 'life chances' available to some are still much better than for others. We look at some of these factors and their impact here and in the next section (pages 60–61).

Families

Families have changed over the past 50 years:

- There are now fewer two-parent nuclear families. Fewer men and women marry and more cohabit (i.e. just live together). Cohabiting relationships are more likely to break up than marriages. Divorce, later marriage and lifestyle choices mean there are now many more one-person households.
- For most people who do marry, marriage comes later in life than it did for their parents. Since the 1969 Divorce Reform Act, divorce has become much easier to obtain, so there are many more divorces and also a significant number of remarriages.
- Since 1971 the proportion of all people living in 'traditional' family households of married couples with dependent children has fallen from half to about a third. Over the same period, the proportion of people living in couples with no children rose from 19% to 25%.
- Nearly a quarter of children lived with just one parent in 2006, and 90% of those households were headed by lone mothers.
- Many more mothers now focus on careers, marrying later, and if they have children they quickly return to work after their birth. The birth rate has fallen, while nursery and childminding businesses have multiplied in number in recent years.
- There are also big economic differences between men and women and between indigenous people and those from ethnic minorities. While UK social mobility is lower than elsewhere in the world, the Economic and Social Research Council claims that the National Lottery has created over 1,900 new millionaires since its launch in 1994, a new and unusual form of social mobility.

Taking it further

Life chances are affected by circumstances as well as by people's attitudes and aspirations. The discussion on culture and socialisation (see pages 70–71) gives you some pointers. Using the search engine on your computer, look at 'life chances' in the context of people with disabilities, ethnic minorities or those discussed in reports of the Social Exclusion Task Force.

Education

Education is the main factor deciding whether or not one is upwardly mobile. There are very unequal success rates at school and unequal entry and success rates in further and higher education.

- Even though many more people gain a degree each year, the increase in the proportion of young people from working-class occupations taking part in higher education is much less than the increase among those from better-off families. In more affluent families getting a degree is an expected part of education, while up until now it has not been part of the experience or expectations of those from more modest circumstances.
- Another reason why some young people from working-class homes may reject the idea of higher education may be because they fear accumulating large debts as a result of the tuition and top-up fees that undergraduates now have to pay. The government has increased the means-tested grants for which poorer students are eligible but, as so often with means-tested benefits, many do not know about them or choose not to apply.
- For those born in the early 1980s inequality of access to university has widened further. The share of people from the poorest 20% of families obtaining a degree has risen from 6% to 9%, but the graduation rates for the richest 20% of families have risen from 20% to 47%.
- So in terms of education and 'life chances', the very rich (incomes above £500,000) are now pulling further away from the merely prosperous. Sadly, if you were born in 1970 into the poorest 25% of the population, there is a 37% chance you'll be staying there; for those born in 1958, there was only a 31% chance of remaining at that level. It's a very depressing trend.

Health

Health inequalities remain stark.

- The poor have the worst physical and mental health and the shortest life expectancy.
- One effect of poverty is the concentration of poorer people into particular areas. Men and women are five times more likely to be permanently sick in the worst-off areas. If attempts to reverse such trends are based on means-tested benefits, experience shows that many will fall through the net.
- An exception to the tendency for illness to be centred on the poor comes with the case of depression, anxiety and stress. These and similar mental health disorders are prevalent among the workaholic better-off, according to writer Oliver James. The government announcement in 2008 for a big increase in numbers of psychological therapists employed by the NHS seems to be a recognition of the urgent need to tackle such illnesses, which are often to be found among some of the most economically productive people in society.

Activity

UK governments use means tests, so that only certain groups (e.g. poor families, pensioners, residents or students) are given certain benefits (e.g. working families tax credit, pensioner credit, housing credit or higher education grants).

The government argues that means testing allows it to focus its financial support on the most needy, whereas universal benefits would mean supporting many people who do not need financial aid.

Critics argue that many people do not apply for means-tested benefits because they either do not know how to apply or do not want to have to tell the government all about their personal affairs. They also argue that if financial support were offered to all in universal benefits without any means testing, then the poorest would benefit without thinking that they were getting 'charity'.

Debate the two sides of the means test argument. What do you think?

Key terms

glass ceiling – refers to situations where the progress of a qualified person, typically a woman, within the hierarchy of an organisation is halted at a particular level because of some form of discrimination, most commonly sexism or racism. The ceiling is glass because the limitation is not immediately apparent and is normally an unwritten and unofficial policy.

Social factors influencing behaviour and life chances 2

To complete our understanding of the changing patterns of 'life chances' we now need to examine factors such as material reward, the position of women, the impact of social exclusion and the role of immigrants and ethnic minorities.

Material reward

In 2004 men were still paid more than women, in spite of the Equal Pay Act having been passed in 1970; however, the gap was the smallest yet. Results from the Annual Survey of Hourly Earnings showed median hourly pay of £11.04 for men and £9.46 for women.

But there remain serious inequalities in Britain:

- The most wealthy 1% own 21% of all UK wealth.
- The least wealthy 50% own only 7% of UK wealth.
- Chief Executives of FTSE 100 (the 100 biggest companies) earn on average £730,796 a year.
- The median UK salary is about £25,000 a year.
- A full-time employee on the minimum wage of £5.52 for over 22s would earn about £10,000 a year.

The position of women

It is said that the pay and promotion available to women are often limited by a **glass ceiling**. Fewer than one in four Members of Parliament or Members of the European Parliament are female (although the devolved bodies in Edinburgh and Cardiff do much better than this in terms of gender equality). About one in six university professors are female but there are fewer than one in ten female judges and company directors and fewer than two in a hundred are chief executives of big companies.

- Women grew as a proportion of the workforce from 29% in 1900 to 46% in 2000. In 2000 there were 13 million women in employment.
- Women are found in particular jobs in the UK labour market: they provide 79% of secretarial and administration workers and 83% of personal service workers.
- But only 9% of skilled trades employees are female and they provide only 31% of managers and senior officials.
- Many women who might have stayed at home to bring up their children are now pressured/helped to gain employment through government schemes such as New Deal.

Social exclusion

Unemployment, homelessness, low pay and poor housing combine to exclude some communities from the mainstream of society. In particular young people who feel alienated and on the 'outside' may embrace anti-social values, form gangs in 'sink' estates and relate mainly to subcultures of their own. The government's Social Exclusion Task Force works on initiatives to tackle these problems. However some people have argued that the introduction of ASBOs (anti-social behaviour orders), which were designed to control and reduce threatening behaviour, has proved instead to be a badge of honour for some young people.

The Economic and Social Research Council has found that youth street gangs in Britain represent a serious social problem. Researchers regard as significant the role of violence and drugs as well as ethnic and religious differences. Many murders and racist attacks on young people in recent years appear to have been carried out by members from different gangs, sometimes fighting over territory.

Immigration

Immigrants to the UK have historically been downwardly mobile. Many first-generation Commonwealth migrants during the 20th century took manual jobs in the UK, having held **white-collar** positions in their country of birth. Doctors and teachers from overseas could get only menial jobs as street cleaners or refuse collectors. However, many new arrivals work hard and once established in this country rapidly improve their social and economic position. In some groups, birth rates among such groups are reversing the long-term trend in the UK for birth rates to fall.

Increasingly most UK citizens are at ease with the idea of living in a multicultural society. Shortages of builders, plumbers, nurses, doctors and dentists in the UK have been alleviated by the arrival of qualified applicants for such jobs from EU or Commonwealth countries. New arrivals from overseas increasingly recognise the need to learn to speak and write English if they are to become integrated in UK society.

After World War II, Britain couldn't get enough workers to help rebuild the economy and to work in the new NHS so employers also looked to Commonwealth countries such as India, South Africa, Kenya, Pakistan and the Caribbean islands, which had strong cultural links with Britain, including language. Many arrived in the hope of building a new life for their young families.

Now the descendants of such immigrants are the teachers, footballers, TV presenters, musicians and politicians who shape British society. There are numerous ethnic newspapers, magazines, TV programmes, radio stations and internet sites for each community. The largest groups live in and around London, and many other groups are concentrated in the industrial centres of Yorkshire, the Midlands and the South East. There are also many new arrivals from Eastern European EU countries such as Poland, Lithuania, Hungary and Slovenia. But rather than focus on where people originated from, there are now growing pressures to emphasise that once people have arrived and settled here, they become British citizens.

Migration patterns to and from the UK are changing. Although up to 600,000 people from other countries come to the UK every year to study or work or for extended holidays, as many as 400,000 leave our country to go and live overseas. In 2008 the government announced that in future immigration will be controlled by a points-based system so that priority will be given to admitting people with qualifications who can fill skill shortages in the UK labour market. There is presently a debate about whether individuals should be required to learn and speak English to gain UK citizenship.

Taking it further

Bodies such as the Sutton Trust and the Economic and Social Research Council monitor aspects of status and social mobility in the UK. If you are planning to take an exam in General Studies you should make sure you are aware of their latest reports on such matters.

Key terms

white collar – refers to the types of jobs undertaken by people in the professions (doctors, lawyers, accountants) or by managers or clerical and administrative workers

Taking it further

Citizenship ceremonies are now organised throughout the country for new British subjects. Contact your local council and find out when and how such ceremonies have been held in your locality.

Examiners' Tips

Always try to use the most up to date figures when you answer exam questions on migration. Social Trends, which can be found on the Office for National Statistics website, is a good source to use.

How attitudes have changed 1: The welfare state, equality and rights

The 1930s had witnessed much social distress, only made worse by the ravages of World War II. When he wrote his report in 1942, Sir William Beveridge, former director of the London School of Economics and Liberal MP, highlighted five giant evils: (1) idleness was seen as a big problem because unemployment had been high; (2) many diseases were life-threatening since healthcare was only good if you were wealthy; (3) housing was largely rented and often inadequate, with squalid conditions in many slums; (4) want or poverty was rife, specially for the elderly whose state pension was barely sufficient; (5) levels of ignorance were high, since many had little education and the school leaving age was 14.

William Beveridge wanted the population to be protected from the 'cradle to the grave'. He believed the state should be social engineers. He was supported by John Maynard Keynes, an influential Cambridge economist. 'Keynesianism' regarded government intervention in the economy as necessary to provide stability. He saw public spending as an important regulator which could be used to stimulate the economy at a time of a slump or to damp down growth if it occurs too quickly.

Beveridge's ideas led to the welfare state, a system involving:

- the establishment of the *National Health Service* (NHS) in 1948;
- *education reforms*, which saw the school leaving age rise to 15 in 1944 and 16 in 1969; the 1944 Butler Act introduced a system of free grammar schools (entry by 11+), secondary modern schools and technical schools;
- a commitment to full *employment* (under 3% jobless) and family allowances;
- the 1946 National Insurance Act implemented Beveridge's proposals for *social security*, providing for compulsory contributions from employers and employees for sickness, unemployment, maternity and widows' benefits and old age pensions, with the government making up any shortfall;
- accelerated programmes of *council housing* to replace homes destroyed by war-time bombing and raise the standards of housing accommodation generally.

Undoubtedly living conditions have improved throughout the UK, although the gaps between richest and poorest (wealth) and highest and lowest earners (income) have not been reduced.

Indeed, the Economic and Social Research Council said that in 2005 the UK was the least 'equal' society in the EU, comparing poorly with Denmark, Sweden, Germany and France. Worldwide, the UK has greater equality of income distribution than the USA but less than Switzerland; the country with the greatest level of inequality is Namibia, while Belarus has the lowest.

Debates about the welfare state

Since the 1940s, there have been furious debates about whether social goals are not better achieved by private, rather than state, provision.

- In the 1950s, the Conservatives set ambitious targets for *housing* to be met by the private not the public sector. Under the Blair Labour government most new housing was to be provided by private developers, although the Brown Labour government seems to want more housing to be provided by councils or housing associations.
- Much *employment* was originally provided in **nationalised industries**. Later, Conservatives resolved to privatise many of these businesses, such as BT and British Gas, so they were not subsidised by taxes and worked harder to become more profitable.
- Up until the 1980s state *pensions* had increased each year in line with inflation (increasing prices) so pensioners did not fall behind. The Conservative government changed the system, linking pensions instead to changes in earnings; this led to smaller pensions increases. Governments have tried to improve the position of poorer pensioners in recent years with a pensioners tax credit. This has led to claims by people who have saved for their old age, but who do not receive the credit, that they are being penalised.
- As *health* costs, waiting lists and hospital infections rose, many people turned to the expensive but responsive services of private medical health companies such as BUPA.
- The Conservative government challenged the idea of *full employment* as the main priority of government policy in the 1980s and 1990s, believing that 'supply side' economic remedies should be pursued, which promoted greater productivity, competitiveness and efficiency. Many jobs were lost as a result.
- *Education* was also exposed to competition. Government funding was organised so that grants to state schools followed the children (fewer children, less funding); Conservatives offered subsidies to parents who preferred to send their children to independent schools such as Rugby.

Human rights

More than 50 years after the welfare state was formed in the UK, most people now see welfare as part of their 'rights'. If denied a 'right' to which individuals believe they are entitled, they will often go to court. Human rights include individuals' rights to life; privacy and family life; health; freedom of expression and religion; be educated; own property; not to be tortured or given degrading punishment.

Disputes over individuals' rights as citizens are resolved in:

- UK courts, following the Human Rights Act 1998, and/or
- the European Court of Human Rights (ECHR, established by the Council of Europe – not part of the EU – in 1950), and/or
- the European Court of Justice which decides matters of EU law.

Recent 'rights' cases included *Copland v UK 2007* in which ECHR upheld the complaint of an employee of Carmarthenshire College that her e-mails and telephone calls were unreasonably scrutinised, ordering compensation and costs to be paid.

How attitudes have changed 2: Commuting and communication

The UK was a very different place in 1945. Commuting (travelling miles to work every day) was virtually unknown in 1945. Most people worked in or near the community in which they lived. Communication took place through face-to-face contact, letter-writing, newspapers, listening to the BBC on the radio and, very occasionally, speaking on the telephone (usually in the red telephone box at the end of the road). Buying and selling was undertaken using cash, cheques and credit (if the purchaser had an account with a particular business).

In the years immediately after World War II:
- there was no internet, e-mails or texting;
- there were only a few TV programmes, and only one channel (BBC1);
- telephones were little used, and there were no mobile phones;
- very few people owned a car and there were no motorways;
- most travel was undertaken by train, bus or bicycle;
- shopping was undertaken in the shop face-to-face, largely without catalogues and definitely without credit or debit cards.

Why did commuting increase?
- As a result of the war, many people had become more aware of travelling to different towns.
- As some traditional industries closed, relocated or reduced their workforce (e.g. coal, some manufacturing and agriculture), people started to travel further distances to get work.
- As car ownership increased, it became easier to travel to jobs further afield, especially if they offered the prospect of better rates of pay.
- As the school leaving age rose, more young people needed to travel to find work which matched their ambitions and abilities.
- As more people gained professional qualifications, they travelled further to work to find promotion opportunities.
- As traffic rose, motorways were constructed which made long-distance commuting an easier experience.

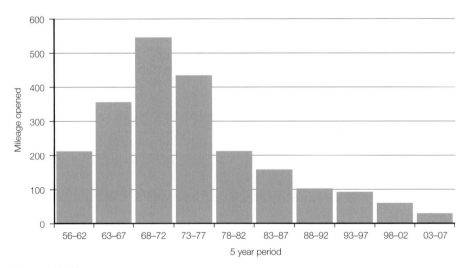

Growth of UK motorways
Between 1959 and 2006 2,211 miles of motorway were constructed in the UK

Changes in the railways

The key point in the decline of UK railways came in the 1960s. As a result of the Beeching Report, many branch lines and stations were closed. Steam trains are rarely used now, except on heritage railway lines, but they make an important contribution to the leisure industry and give a big boost to tourism in areas where they have been restored and re-established.

As road congestion and concern for the environment has increased there has been a strong move towards light tram systems such as the Croydon Tram and Manchester Metro – often constructed using former railway lines. Park and ride schemes and integrated bus/rail links are increasingly popular to make the use of public transport easier and more convenient. As railway infrastructure has been improved, new rolling stock introduced and platforms lengthened, more passengers are now using railways (and in some cases winning business from low-cost air carriers). Using Eurostar travelling at 186mph, London-Paris now takes 2 hours 15 mins, London-Brussels 1 hour 51 mins and London-Lille just 1 hour 20 mins.

Demand for public transport has increased as people are discouraged from using cars in city centres through congestion charges and similar road pricing schemes and because they wish to reduce their carbon footprint.

Technology, communication and equality

If interactivity in the 1940s and 1950s barely reached beyond the telephone at the end of the road, consider how many more ways there are now for people to make contact or keep in touch:

- Many more people now have telephones in their own home so they can speak to or fax people worldwide at relatively little cost. They have mobiles too, which means we need never be out of touch with friends, family or customers.
- There are now innumerable digital television (and radio) stations – including commercial stations carrying advertising – which encourage responses (e.g. 'please push the red button') from listeners and viewers.
- Television and the internet give us access to worldwide markets to buy and sell (e.g. on EBay) and share our own view of the world through blogs and the comments we offer on others' websites.
- GPS equipment means that anyone from motorists to round-the-world travellers can stay in touch and be guided safely to their destination.
- Equality may have proved elusive in many respects, but since most people outside repressive regimes such as China can gain access to the Internet cheaply and easily in an Internet café, technology permits the vast majority – from silver surfer to young entrepreneur – to keep in touch with the rest of the world whenever they want to buy, sell, advertise or simply share ideas.

Taking it further

To understand the extent of closures which followed the Beeching Report, see: www.joyce.whitchurch. btinternet.co.uk/maps.htm Do you think more new railways now need to be constructed? If so, how would you justify that?

Examiners' Tips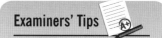

Examiners are always interested in candidates' opinions, but you will get more marks for stating them if you back them up with reasons, evidence or support from known experts/authorities.

Chapter 6 Summary

By now, you should have knowledge and understanding of:

1 How far genetic factors influence behaviour and life chances

- How nature and nurture affect behaviour and life chances.
- The importance of the perspectives of sociologists and biologists.
- Manipulating human genes can lead to intense ethical debates.

2 How social factors dictate life changes and social mobility

- The widening gap which has arisen between children from poorer and better off homes in terms of gaining degrees and professional jobs.
- The inequalities in health which impact on life expectancy.
- How immigrants have demonstrated the ability to establish themselves successfully in the country.

3 Ways in which society has changed; more equal, more multicultural

- The contributions of William Beveridge and John Maynard Keynes to the development of a welfare state.
- Migration patterns to and from our country and how our society is becoming genuinely multicultural.
- While real improvements have been made, the gap between rich and poor remains little changed; also how social exclusion has arisen and the dangers it presents.

4 How and why family life has changed

- The changing characteristics of family life: fewer marriages, lower birth rate, more divorce and remarriages.
- How women now focus on their careers and delay or abstain from having children; the limited extent to which women have been able to break through the glass ceiling.
- The positive contribution to the birth rate by immigrants to the country, though the UK continues to have an ageing population.

5 The impact of having a welfare state for 50 years and the importance of human rights

- The expansion in provision of education and training, health, pensions, social security and housing.
- The role of the private sector in providing such services.
- The increased focus on human rights.

6 The significance of massive changes to work, transport and communication

- The tendency for people to work further from home and to commute regularly by car, train or bus.
- The growth of congestion, which is increasingly combated by more emphasis on public transport and new devices such as road pricing and congestion charges.
- Massive changes in communication, e.g. mobile phones, the Internet and credit/debit cards.

Chapter 7 Where do our values and opinions come from?

What you're going to learn:

- The sources, nature and importance of cultural values
- How far cultural values are shared throughout society
- The different forms and significance of socialisation
- Key elements of social and economic life in the UK
- The extent and significance of mono and multiculturalism, anti-discrimination and freedom of information legislation.

DON'T PANIC, DON'T PANIC – BUT STILL THEY PANIC!

In 2007, the media publicised problems at the Northern Rock Building Society. People's first reaction was to keep their savings safe; they seemed to completely ignore the reassurances from politicians and economists. So they queued up to withdraw their money and often encouraged their friends and relatives to do the same. Is this an emotional rather than a rational response?

Customers queue outside Northern Rock bank in September 2007

Our emotions and what we learn when we are young often form a key part of our opinions, loyalties, values and 'who we trust' later in life, even when our own circumstances may have greatly changed. So our responses are often emotional rather than rational.

Suppose you really like a particular health drink. But your parents say it carries health dangers. The teachers say it is addictive and will reduce your ability to remember things. Television advertisements say it is dangerous and newspapers claim that people of your age have committed suicide after drinking just a few glasses. However, singers in your favourite groups and actresses in your favourite soap are pictured happily drinking it. Your friends like it and say the campaigns against it are just invented by makers who want you to purchase their drinks instead. Are you likely to continue drinking it? *Which, if any, of these influences is most likely to cause you to change your behaviour and drink less of the health drink or give it up altogether?* Your answer will depend partly on your emotions and partly on loyalties for peer groups (friends and equals) and reference groups (authority figures whom you respect).

Activity

In groups, consider the various ways in which life in different parts of the UK maintains its differences. Think about language and dialect, income and wealth, the impact of religions, patterns of employment, sport, entertainment and leisure pursuits.

Key terms

Protestant ethic
(sometimes called the Puritan work ethic) – a term first coined by Max Weber to emphasise the importance of continual work and effort in a person's endeavours leading to personal salvation

ladder of opportunity
– a term coined by Elie Halevy to explain the influence of Methodism on the stability of English society during the late 18th and 19th centuries, whereby it offered a ladder of opportunity to respectable members of the lower orders, and helped prevent the social polarisation of English society in the wake of industrialisation

Taking it further

What other religions (if any) have had an impact on cultural values in the UK?

Society as culture: cultural values and where they come from

Culture is the distinctive way of life conducted by an entire community or society, including codes of manners, dress, language, religion, rituals, norms of behaviour concerning law and morality, and systems of belief. Cultural activities such as art, dance or poetry often reflect the changing patterns and experiences that people encounter within their society.

Although there are many differences that occur within society, communication technology brings us all closer together to create a society that is increasingly homogeneous. Consider how characteristic features associated with particular parts of our country are now less visible. Once every high street in the UK was distinctive and different; now it is often difficult to know whether you are in Northampton or Southampton, Eastbourne or Westbury.

What do we mean by 'cultural values' and where do they come from?

Cultural values and their sources are very personal and individual. They are born out of our history and traditions, the insights of writers and historians, and to some extent Britain's changing role in the world as we move from the days of empire as a proud island race to become a key power in a modern Europe. There are some broad truths that can be identified:

- Many of us identify with a country or a place, which we regard with loyalty and often nostalgia – a very special kind of patriotism
- We pride ourselves on having a sense of fairness as befits free people living in a democracy where every man or woman is as entitled as the next to express an opinion
- This is coupled with an unwillingness to stand silently by as tyrants bully the weak; examples are Hitler's invasion of Poland; the break-up of former Yugoslavia; and the genocide in Rwanda, Sierra Leone and Darfur in Africa
- In our personal lives, certainties over ethical and moral issues – marriage, divorce, abortion, adoption, suicide, sexual preference – have been eroded to become uncertainties for some
- We know too that society permits inequalities, which mean some people live on low incomes in inadequate housing, often with poor health and with little possibility of improving their situation
- Some condemn a focus on materialism as a contemporary selfishness
- Other people share an optimism derived from religion – whether Max Weber's **Protestant ethic** or the Methodist-inspired **ladder of opportunity**.

People tend to disagree which of these values and beliefs are most significant at any one time. Sir John Major, a former prime minister, summed up his view in 1993 by saying:

Fifty years from now, Britain will still be the country of long shadows on county grounds, warm beer, invincible green suburbs, dog lovers and pools fillers and – as George Orwell said – 'old maids cycling to holy communion through the morning mist'...

A very different view was expressed by journalist Jeremy Paxman in his 1998 book *The English*:

> *The English wear baseball caps and jeans, eat versions of American, Asian or Italian food, drive cars made anywhere on the globe (even the grandest British car-maker is now owned by Germans), dance to international beats and play computer games designed in Seattle or Tokyo … neither geography nor history, religion nor politics exerts the influence it once did. And as external fashions have changed in the last half-century, so too have the internal certainties. The Second World War, the time of* Brief Encounter *and* In Which We Serve*, was the last extended period when we could say with any confidence that the impression of England matched the reality.*

New perspectives on society and values

Different influences are at work on different generations, helping to explain changing opinions, tastes in music or dress and changing forms of language (e.g. the influence of texting on traditional syntax and spellings).

- There is less deference in society now and many more people are willing to reject previously supported conventions.
- In the past, many workers looked for the security of working for one firm for the whole of their working life. Now increasingly people change jobs and accept a whole series of short-term contracts with different employers; this may seem a riskier strategy, but as more workers now have better qualifications, people have greater confidence in their ability to change their lives.
- Many fewer people now aim to live in a nuclear family with mum, dad and two children. People are also now much more open about their sexual orientation (given that male homosexuality was illegal until 1967) so more people may now choose to live in a civil partnership with a same-sex partner, or cohabit with a different-sex partner, or live as a single person, perhaps entering into a relationship later in life.
- As many more jobs are now opened up to women or workers from overseas, so values in the workplace have changed.

Britain can look and feel very different in different geographical locations thanks to the distinctly different attitudes and values held by different sub-cultures:

- There are mining areas or fishing ports which have a sense of togetherness and solidarity which is clearly culturally based; sometimes even former mining areas sustain the same sense of shared goals, 'family' and community.
- Major differences in values and lifestyles have always been evident in villages or more isolated rural communities when compared to suburbs and inner cities.
- Under 25s often speak and text in a vocabulary parents scarcely understand; their tastes in music and clothes, their values and the people they look up to are often different from those of the teenagers of ten years ago.
- We are close to having several 'plural cities' now in Britain (e.g. Leicester and Birmingham) where no ethnic group will be in a majority (including whites). Many different minorities make invaluable multicultural contributions of their own to create a distinctive sub-cultural mix.

Activity

Discuss which five features of 'your' Britain (or England, Wales or Scotland, if you prefer) best highlight contemporary cultural values. Try to identify one or two values which you now consider significantly less important than you once did – and explain why.

The impact of socialisation on identities, self-images and culture

Socialisation is the process by which we learn the behaviour, values and attitudes considered appropriate in the culture and society in which we live. It is through socialisation that we gain a sense of identity and, hence, learn the roles we need to fulfil within our country or community. In exercising these roles, we build up a self-image of our proper place in the society.

The differences between primary and secondary socialisation and their significance

Primary socialisation is when people learn attitudes, values and actions appropriate to individuals as members of a particular culture. It largely occurs in the family during the early years of childhood, when the child learns about, absorbs and accepts the culture of its society. The long-term continuance of social life would be in doubt if the child did not internalise (make their own) such shared norms and social values as part of her or his personality structure.

A key issue for societies is the problem that if families are the principal agents of primary socialisation, what happens when families break down?

Secondary socialisation typically occurs later, when the family is less central than the influence of school or work or leisure. The learning of appropriate behaviour as a member of a smaller group (sub-culture) within the larger society is undertaken at school or via peer groups.

In the past, attendance at church services and church-organised activities such as Sunday schools was a significant source of secondary socialisation. As such attendances have declined this has become a less important influence, except for the families of children in ethnic minorities who are generally perceived as being more devout, for example the many families from EU countries who now attend Roman Catholic services in the UK or the many Muslim families.

Inevitably, therefore, those pupils who relate badly to school or who fail to attend regularly are very likely to have a narrow or distorted view of society and this may contribute to any apparently anti-social behaviour they may exhibit.

The importance of coherence, consistency and reliability in establishing roles

In primary socialisation, parents provide role models for their children, so they learn appropriate behaviour for both sexes. If children are to understand such roles, the parents need to maintain the essential characteristics of the role in a consistent manner, so the child does not feel any sense of arbitrariness (i.e. sometimes this applies, sometimes not). By the time this stage of the socialisation process has been completed, the child needs to be confident about their parents' and also their own role and place in the family and society. Children brought up in single parent households may consequently be put at a disadvantage in preparing for their role as an adult in society. However, the evidence is not conclusive. Amelia Hill argued (in *The Observer*, 25 February 2001) that bad behaviour such as petty vandalism, drug taking, drinking, smoking and mixing with the wrong crowd was just as likely to be the actions of middle-class teenagers from two-parent families as of working-class children from broken homes.

Although the role played by parents is likely to diminish in secondary socialisation as the child gets older, particular problems occur if the parents' influence on the child is greatly reduced through divorce or separation or perhaps because the parent is being employed out of the home for much of the time when the child is not at school. The 2006 report of the Social Justice Policy group saw 'dadlessness' as being hugely important in explaining bad behaviour.

Lack of parental influence may lead to the child being disproportionately influenced by peer groups or school friends, or by those with whom the child plays particular sports. Such influences can be positive and helpful in assisting the child to learn appropriate patterns of behaviour and may impact positively and beneficially on their self-image and behaviour. This is especially the case if the school or the sports team gives structure to their life and/or a sense of empowerment (awareness that they can 'make a difference'), thus giving them a responsible role to fulfil.

However, if other influences are absent for some reason, the child might make inappropriate identifications and drift into gang membership, drug use, heavy drinking or use of knives, which may be linked to fans of particular sports teams or pop groups. One finding of 'Fractured Families', the 2007 interim report of the Family Breakdown Working Group, was that children of 'neglectful parents' are more likely to suffer impaired psychological development and be at increased risk of drug and alcohol abuse and delinquency.

A child who identifies with the norms of society as a result of strong parental influences at the primary socialisation stage and through positive influences via peer groups and school at the secondary stage will be self-confident, having acquired a strong set of 'benchmarks' which will help to ensure the youngster is less likely to drift into trouble. Problems arise in cases where such strong influences have not been established or the underlying social norms have not been internalised. Identities may also be linked to class, fashion, a particular part of the country, religion, race or ethnicity, gender or economic circumstances such as employment (high or low pay) or unemployment (poor self-image, sense of hopelessness). What is important is that the growing child has acquired, understands and shares society's 'rules of the game'.

Perhaps a bigger problem still was identified in a 2002 study of 12,000 students, as reported by Gaby Hinsliff in *The Observer* (14 April 2002). Research showed that instead of one-parent families being guilty of creating problem teenagers, the key factor may instead be workaholic or distant parents with no time to listen to older children. This problem poses a greater threat, since the children are denied the support they need to internalise the values and identifications which can ensure they enter society as responsible, balanced adults.

Taking it further

Organise a simple questionnaire among fellow students or your friends at any sports clubs you go to. Can you find a link between their socialisation and the self-image they have? What values do they hold and how do they see their role in society? Are answers from young men in line with those from young women?

Living in the UK

In this section we are concerned with employment, unemployment, the economy, mono and multiculturalism, anti-discrimination and the nature and impact of freedom of information legislation.

Employment and unemployment

Living standards in the UK in future years could take a sharp turn downwards as more and more workers reach retirement age. Indigenous UK birth rates have fallen sharply in recent decades; there will therefore be a shortage of workers to produce the national income on which standards of living depend, unless drastic action is taken. Recent governments have worked hard to get more people into the labour market by:

- *raising activity rates* by getting women to go to work rather than stay at home. One in two mothers of under fives are now in the labour force, thanks to improved child-minding provision. Working age women with dependent children are still less likely to be economically active than those without children – 68% compared with 76% in spring 2003 – but the number of women working is up by 10–15% since the 1980s. Women are more likely than men to work part time.
- *raising retirement ages* to reflect the greater life expectancy in 21st century Britain. This means that men who continue working can receive a bonus on their state pension if they delay drawing it until after the age of 65 (or 60 for women). The state retirement age, which is set to be 65 for both men and women by 2020, will rise to 66 between 2024 and 2026, to 67 between 2034 and 2036 and to 68 between 2044 and 2046.

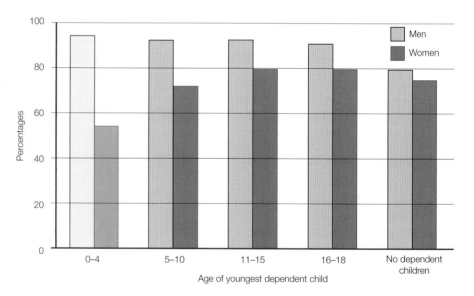

Work and family – economic activity by men and women in the UK labour market (2003) by age of youngest dependent child (www.ons.gov.uk)

For the reasons explained above, the proportion of those in the UK seeking work who are actually unemployed is much lower than in many other EU countries. The unemployment rate in June 2007 was 5.4% in the UK compared to 8.3% in Germany, 8.5% in Spain, 9.5% in France, 13.4% in Slovakia and 13.9% in Poland.

The economy

Inflation means rising prices and deflation falling prices. The price of something we buy may go up for various reasons:

- because people are competing to buy it (e.g. a house or a painting)
- because wages have risen (e.g. the national minimum wage)
- because the product was made abroad and imported into the UK; so if the price used to be 10 Euros when the exchange rate was 2 Euros = £1 (i.e. price = £5) the price will go up to £6.66 if the exchange rate becomes £1 = 1.5 Euros. (Moving exchange rates also affect the prices we receive when we export goods overseas.)

If prices go up, we may save less or borrow more. How much we receive from our savings depends on the rate of interest paid. We can be sure, though, that if we are paid 4% or 5% on our savings, we shall have to pay at least 6%, 7% or 8% on any borrowing that we do through loans or credit cards; that is how the bank or building society makes a profit and keeps going. The higher interest rates go, the fewer businesses will make new investments; yet firms which fail to invest are failing to innovate and keep abreast of the latest technologies, and thus may lose trade to their competitors.

Stakeholder, occupational and private pensions (as opposed to state pensions) often invest contributions from the employee or the employer in investments and shares, so if the profits are good, the individual will receive a better pension on retirement.

Taxes raised by government from individuals are 'indirect' if not collected directly from the individual (e.g. VAT on things we buy) or 'direct' if we know we are paying the tax (e.g. income tax). Government spending is called public sector expenditure, whereas spending by a private firm or club is called private sector expenditure. If the government wants to support an organisation, they may pay them a subsidy or grant.

How open and equal is society in the UK?

The UK has become more open and equal in the past 20 years, but not as much as many would wish. If 'information is power', then people are now more powerful as a result of the Freedom of Information Act 2000, which has greatly reduced secrecy.

However, many people fear their privacy is being eroded as a result of the so-called 'surveillance society', in which every time we go out our photo might be taken by closed-circuit television cameras, or our spending tracked through the use of credit and debit cards

The greater emphasis on citizens' rights and responsibilities means there have been real improvements in both kinds of freedom – positive (freedom to …) and negative (freedom from …). Many areas of discrimination have been tackled by anti-discrimination laws dealing with gender, homosexuality, disability, race and age. The Equal Pay Act 1970 was passed to equalise the pay of men and women who do identical work; pay may still be unequal, but less so than used to be the case. Other forms of discrimination are combated by the new Commission for Equality and Human Rights, which works against discrimination on the basis of race, age, gender and disability.

Taking it further

Look at www.equalityhumanrights.com, the Commission for Equality and Human Rights website, and follow through some of the recent cases they report there. This will give you up-to-date examples for your General Studies exam.

Chapter 7 Summary

By now, you should have knowledge and understanding of:

1 The sources, nature and importance of cultural values

- Culture as the distinctive way of life for an entire community or society.
- The impact of different traditions as sources of such values.
- The balance between ethical, moral, religious, social and historic inputs.

2 How far cultural values are shared throughout society

- The interplay between cultural values and widespread changes in the way society works.
- A recognition of the extent and significance of sub-cultures.
- The significance of the emergence of 'plural cities' in Britain.

3 The different forms and significance of socialisation

- The key characteristics of primary socialisation and the significance of 'dadlessness'.
- The changing patterns of secondary socialisation.
- The significance of religion as an influence on behaviour.

4 Key elements of social and economic life in the UK

- The government's strategies for improving economic activity rates.
- The changing contribution of women to the labour market.
- The nature of the economy (and particularly employment and unemployment) in Britain compared to other European Union countries.

5 The extent and significance of mono and multiculturalism, anti-discrimination and freedom of information legislation

- The increase in multiculturalism as many people from other countries come to live and work in the UK.
- The increase in transparency of economic and social life contrasted with an increasing loss of privacy.
- The greater emphasis now given to monitoring and minimising discrimination.

Chapter 8 Mass media: representation or reality?

What you're going to learn:

- Local, national and global forms of the media
- The impact of censorship and other constraints
- the influence of the audience on the media and society

Media is a term we all know – but what does it mean? It covers many different areas. Broadcasting and print are important forms of media, but the list also includes electronic media and film. Print media, the original form of mass media, includes newspapers, books and magazines. The common link between them is that they all transmit information to a mass audience through the written or printed word. Other written media (personal letters, postcards or diaries) communicate on an individual basis. Broadcasting includes radio and television. It was the development of radio in the 1920s that introduced the term **mass media**. Electronic media (including the Internet) also allows mass communication. Other media types include film, video, CDs and DVDs.

Media industries are concerned with the transmission and storage of information. Controllers of the media shape what is transmitted, so that the audience receives the information owners wish to convey. Many commentators believe that the media has too much influence.

It is easy to confuse the medium (or method of communication) with the message (that which is being communicated). It may help if you think about electricity. The cable which carries the supply from the generator to the consumer is the medium. Electricity, which is what the consumer wants, is the message. Message and medium are very different but are equally dependent on each other.

Key terms

media – the methods or agents of communication between groups of people, using visual, verbal or written means; media is sometimes used to describe the industries which produce material as well as the methods of transmission.
mass media – the use of technology to communicate with large audiences simultaneously

Activity

Pictures like the one on the left are printed regularly in the media. Is their purpose simply to inform or to shape emotions?

Examiners' Tips

Media is a plural word (the correct singular form is 'medium') but increasingly it is treated as a collective noun. It is just as correct to write 'the media is …' as to write the more traditionally acceptable 'the media are …'.

Local, national and global forms of the media

Globalisation is a major development linked to the growth of mass media. The Internet and satellite television mean events anywhere in the world are witnessed by millions as they occur. Electronic media allows more information to be stored and to be instantly available than ever before. For example, googling 'media' will produce 'about 1,820,000,000 hits in 0.06 seconds'.

The power of the media

The media has considerable power and influence. For many people it is their main source of information. It shapes our world view of events, but often what are presented as facts are really opinions. Inevitably the mass media can shape the way we think. This means that the owners and producers of the media can possess great power.

Individuals or groups which own media outlets (like television stations or newspapers) determine the 'spin' its output has. They dictate to producers or editors how information is presented. Editorial control influences:

- the selection of news stories that are or are not reported
- the amount of time and space given to each story
- the way a story is presented
- the language or images which are used to support the story
- the importance given to a story by its placement
- the way an audience interprets a story.

Media bias and control

Bias clearly exists in all forms of the media. Many of us subconsciously welcome and invite media bias. We select newspapers or television programmes that match our own interests. This is one practical explanation of why there are so many different newspapers, magazines and television programmes: each appeals to a specific target audience. There are differences between the attitudes and values of each newspaper. Traditionally there has been a distinction between 'quality' and 'popular' newspapers. *The Telegraph* and *The Guardian* are 'quality' newspapers but appeal to different interests and present news and opinion with different biases. Similarly *The Sun* and *The Mirror*, as popular newspapers, adopt different approach to stories. Most newspapers have recognisable political loyalties which can change if it suits the owner.

The media can exercise significant influence by the way it shapes and presents news and information. Editors play a crucial role in this. They usually follow a line approved by the owners but can mould news and so create a news agenda. Media bias, however, not only reflects the attitudes of owners and producers but also audience demands. If we don't like something we won't read or view it.

The UK press is not restricted by law, but there is an independent body called the Press Complaints Commission (PCC) which deals with complaints from the public about newspaper and magazine content. Broadcasting and other telecommunication are controlled by Ofcom, established by the Office of Communications Act 2002. Ofcom monitors the media to ensure impartiality and to restrict bias. It is said to have too wide a range of responsibilities to

Key terms

globalisation – how the world population has been unified into a single society; the development of worldwide social and economic ties

Examiners' Tips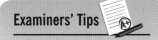

Arguments are stronger if you can give specific examples of media owners or producers rather than discuss them in general terms.

Taking it further

Examine reports of an event carried by different newspapers and compare headlines and reporting styles. Is there evidence of (a) overt (open) and (b) covert (hidden) bias?

Activity

Investigate either reports of the PCC or Ofcom adjudications on complaints about biased reporting. How effective was the judgement? What powers do regulatory bodies have to sanction offenders?

function effectively, but it is an attempt to control the media in the interests of the public. It has statutory and regulatory duties and is required to:

- ensure a wide range of TV and radio services of high quality and wide appeal
- maintain plurality in the provision of broadcasting
- adequately protect audiences against offensive or harmful material
- adequately protect audiences against unfairness or the infringement of privacy.

The BBC Charter and ITV Television Acts impose the duty of impartiality on the broadcast media. This requirement is not made of other forms of media.

Remember that both broadcast and print media offer entertainment as well as news. These are just as much subject to media bias and probably influence viewers or readers more because they do not overtly present information.

The media and wider issues

In 1972 Stan Cohen suggested that the media could create concern or 'moral panics' over social issues. He argued that the way it reports and responds to unacceptable behaviour can define it in the minds of readers. This could legitimise a pattern of behaviour encouraging others to copy it. He suggested that the media by the way it reports behaviours actually causes these behaviours to increase and so creates greater public concern ('moral panics'), partly by identifying hate figures ('folk devils'). Recently there have been many areas of social concern that some have seen as moral panics, including:

- anti-Islamic feeling
- illegal immigration
- paedophilia
- teenage pregnancy
- knife crime
- hospital super-bugs.

The media has an important role in raising awareness of social issues and helping to change public attitudes. Soap operas such as *Coronation Street*, *East Enders*, *Emmerdale* or *The Archers* examine a wide range of issues. Ideas of tolerance, understanding, informed awareness, sympathy and acceptability can be created where previously they may not have existed. Topics covered include:

- moral issues (e.g. divorce, sexuality, abortion and euthanasia)
- health issues (e.g. cancer, physical and mental disabilities, AIDs and drugs)
- social problems (e.g. homelessness, unemployment, single parents and violence.

Remember that the media can only reach and influence people willing to be reached. The 'off-switch' is a powerful weapon with which to resist influence.

> **Taking it further**
>
> Research theories about moral panics. What arguments are there to (a) support and (b) challenge the strength of Cohen's claims?

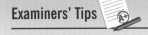
Censorship and other constraints

One of the most debated issues about the mass media is whether or not **censorship** is justified. It is important to recognise the different types of censorship: government-imposed or controlled censorship, authoritarian censorship and self-censorship. In each case censorship may be formal or informal. The essence of censorship, whichever type is considered, is that a restriction is imposed on the free transmission of information.

Types of censorship

Generally, when discussing censorship, we think of government restrictions. Do not assume that only totalitarian governments use censorship. Most of us know that the Chinese government has restrictive controls over the Internet, but we can forget that most governments use some forms of censorship. In the UK formal government censorship exists in wartime, but less formal methods are used in peacetime, often operating through independent regulatory bodies such as the PCC, Ofcom or the British Board of Film Classification.

These regulatory bodies often carry out 'after-the-event' censorship since they usually deal with complaints after publication rather than censor material before it is published. Decisions are based on agreed codes of practice or ultimately appeals to the law. The British Board of Film Classification is rather different, since it issues age certificates for films and videos. However, local authorities have statutory power to overturn these recommendations.

Authoritarian censorship is when positions of power are used to limit access to information. Media owners and editors can exercise this type of censorship. Everyday examples of authoritarian censors are teachers and parents who use their position to decide what individuals under their care can see or read.

Self-censorship is when individuals decide for themselves the information they will receive. An example of self-censorship is when you switch off the television or stop reading because you do not want to be offended.

Arguments for and against censorship

Justifications for censorship include:

- to protect the security of the state and maintain morale
- to prevent an enemy learning information that might harm the war effort
- to prevent children being exposed to violence
- to protect people from being corrupted by overt sexuality
- to protect the government (or a political group or individual) from being weakened by the release of sensitive information or by criticism
- to protect people from misinformation
- to protect individual privacy.

Arguments against censorship include:

- people need accurate information in order to make sound choices
- censorship is an infringement of individual liberty
- adults ought to decide for themselves what they wish to see or read
- freedom of speech is a fundamental right
- censors do not seem to be corrupted by offensive material
- no one has the right to decide what somebody else should see or read
- it has not been proved that media material may corrupt or deprave
- access to the Internet has made censorship ineffective.

Other constraints on the media

Defamation is a serious matter and the mass media usually seeks to avoid it. Editors and publishers check the legal status of material before publishing. People suffering defamation are protected by **libel** and **slander** laws and can sue offenders. Enormous damages can be awarded but judges can also grant minimal damages for trivial claims. Laws designed to protect the rights of the individual and restrict media freedom to publish what they choose include:

- The Official Secrets Act 1989 forbids publication of secrets harmful to the state.
- The Human Rights Acts 1998 and 2000 protect privacy against media intrusion.
- The Blasphemy Act 1697 bans offences against religion. Recently it has proved ineffective and governments recognise the need for reform.

Unfortunately, these laws only come into operation once an offence has been committed, but fear of legal action may restrain media producers from publishing unacceptable material. Too often, when the law is used, damage and harm has already occurred.

The Freedom of Information Act 2005 allows the public access to information held by public authorities. Some provisions apply to public service broadcasters. There has been much discussion about the need for privacy laws. Several high-profile court cases have revealed that the media appear more concerned to attract customers than to respect the rights of individuals.

UK media are also subject to laws relating to decency and pornography. The Obscene Publications Acts 1959 and 1964 define obscenity and can be used to censor potentially offensive material. It is not normally an offence for adults to own or possess pornographic material, but it is an offence to publish it. Child pornography is child abuse and so is illegal in the UK. The Internet is proving to be a real problem as far as pornography in the media is concerned, as it is a global agent and so is difficult to control or censor.

Voluntary controls on the media

Another effective form of censorship, the news blackout, occurs when the media are asked not to publish sensitive material which may hinder criminal investigations. It can be harmful if governments or media owners use it for their own private purposes. Easy access to the Internet, where unscrupulous people can publish any material they choose, even when it is not allowed to appear in print or be broadcast, has made it possible to ignore such censorship.

Since 1971 five standing DA (Defence Advisory) notices give guidance on what can and cannot be published. DA notices are official government requests not to publish material which may endanger national security. They are voluntary and have sometimes been ignored by editors 'in the public interest'. Subsequent prosecutions have used the Official Secrets Act.

The 'watershed' is a voluntary control. Broadcasters agree that 'adult content' will not be shown before 9.00pm, after which time it is assumed impressionable children will be in bed. However, there is an increasing tendency for these restrictions to be interpreted too broadly or even be ignored.

The influence of audiences on the media

Recent developments in audience participation have changed the nature of the media. 'Readers' letters' have always been a feature of newspapers. Programmes like *Points of View* and *Any Answers* have a similar role in broadcasting. Readers and viewers could express opinions but not participate significantly in the structure of content.

Today we have much greater opportunity to contribute to media output. In an updating of the traditional letters page, online newspapers encourage readers' comments and participation in discussions.

Developments in broadcasting have been dramatic. Digital broadcasting allows viewers to choose which of several different screens to watch. For example, Sky News simultaneously provides eight different screens and eight text programmes. Other news services offer similar but more limited provision. More significantly, viewers can express opinions by voting or commenting on topical issues as well as participating in on-air discussions. This has both curtailed and increased the role of the news editor. Viewers have greater choice, but a broader range of material must be available. Sports channels offer similar selections of matches with opportunities for interactive participation.

The influence of phone-in shows

Most media companies use phone-in shows. These are relatively inexpensive to produce, draw substantial audiences, attract significant advertising revenue and generate considerable additional revenue. Apparently unlimited cash prizes on shows like *Who Wants To Be a Millionaire?* are almost all generated from prospective contestants' phone calls. Further income is generated from spin-off merchandise and sales of broadcasting rights to other countries.

In 2007 the broadcast media were rocked by phone-in scandals. Millions of viewers were defrauded through high-profile programmes which encouraged them to make premium-rate phone calls to competitions or phone-in polls, even though they had no chance of winning or having their votes counted. Sometimes phoney winners were invented and results falsified. Ofcom imposed massive fines and for a time phone-in programmes were taken off air. In early 2008 Ofcom issued tighter regulations claiming, 'Viewers must be confident of being treated fairly and consistently when interacting with television programmes.' Ofcom's powers have been increased to help combat editorial abuses.

Viewers like phone-in and reality shows because they feel involved as 'ordinary' people in unscripted situations, making an input to programmes. A key feature of many programmes is that viewers are encouraged to take part in increasingly bizarre or demeaning activities. Some experimental drama or entertainment programmes have offered viewers a choice of different endings.

The power of the Internet

We are no longer passive receivers of the media and are not restricted to making our views known anonymously or through face to face confrontation, although this can still bring about public awareness and social change. In the 2001 general election campaign Prime Minister Blair was publicly challenged by Sharon Storer about inadequate Health Service funding and cancer care. Her face-to-face protest was more effective because it was broadcast in the media. The development of the Internet, more than any other technological change, has helped empower individuals. This was illustrated by responses to a petition on the Prime Minister's website which forced the government to change policy over road pricing.

Blogging is a popular and influential way for the public to exercise their voice, distribute ideas, shape news and create opinions. Creating a **blog** does not require any specialist equipment or technological expertise. Material can be posted instantaneously and readers can post comments and responses. The term blog was first used in 1997, although the practice had been evolving slowly since 1983. Blogging has taken off since 1999 and it is estimated that there are over 100 million active bloggers worldwide (with another 200 million 'retired' bloggers). There is no effective control over what is posted, which is very much the product of an individual's personality. Today, as well as ordinary people, bloggers include broadcasters, entertainers, business people and politicians. Blogs can lead to problems, especially for totalitarian regimes.

Funding the media

This is a significant issue in a free society. It is undesirable for the media to be state funded, as this can give politicians too much power and influence. Occasionally, especially during crises, governments will finance and produce their own newspapers. In the 1926 General Strike *The British Gazette,* edited by Winston Churchill, proved a highly biased instrument of government propaganda. It illustrated the importance of a free press in a free society. The BBC, a publicly funded organisation, receives much of its income through the licence fee. This is fixed by government and paid by viewers as a tax, but the BBC prides itself on independence from government control.

Private ownership is an alternative to government funding. Certain individuals and business corporations own substantial sections of the media.

The media (both broadcast and print) is largely financed by advertising revenue. This may give advertisers too much control over content. **Product placement** is an insidious form of advertising. However, the rise of the Internet has challenged traditional media monopoly and attracted much media revenue. Broadcasting is particularly affected by this trend and must look for alternative sources of income, hence the popularity of phone-in shows.

Key terms

blog (or weblog) – an online diary or journal containing text, audio, images or videos; as a verb it means to maintain or add content to web pages.

product placement – when a product's brand or logo is shown as part of a programme, with the production comany receiving a fee

Taking it further

Identify problems associated with blogging. Why might blogging present problems to (a) any government, (b) a totalitarian regime, (c) ordinary citizens? How should it be controlled?

Activity

Discuss to what extent the BBC is genuinely independent of government control. Should an institution funded by the state reflect the values and opinions of the government, or should it have the freedom to reflect all points of view?

Examiners' Tips

Don't confuse control of the media with ownership. Government can control the media through regulations, laws, codes of practice and regulatory bodies, even though it may not actually 'own' the media.

Chapter 8 Summary

By now, you should have knowledge and understanding of:

1 Local, national and global forms of the media

- What the term 'media' means, the different forms of the media and what the differences are between media and mass media.
- Whether government regulation and control of the media is desirable and which institutions are used to enforce such control.
- How and why the media are able to influence the thinking of ordinary people.
- The power of the media, media owners and media bias.
- The way in which the media collectively can create moral panics and the effect these can have on society.
- The way the media use programmes such as soap operas to challenge values and inform as well as entertain.

2 The impact of censorship and other constraints

- The meaning of censorship and the different types of formal and informal censorship used in the UK.
- Arguments for and against the use of media censorship and how different circumstances can affect whether censorship is justified.
- The use of legislation in censorship; the laws that impose restrictions on the media and their potential disadvantages for ordinary people.
- Freedom of information and the right to privacy; alongside the steps that have been taken to balance the rights of the individual against the public's desire to be informed.

3 The influence of the audience on the media and society

- Recent developments in technology which have given audiences the opportunity for greater participation in the media; different forms of interactive media.
- How the Internet has had a major impact on the availability of information and has challenged and changed the role of the traditional media, especially in terms of advertising revenue, accessibility and editorial control.
- The role of editors in shaping news and formulating the news agenda; to what extent they use their power as a response to audience demands or owners' instructions.
- The nature and importance of media owners and the control they exercise.
- How the media is funded.

Chapter 9 Do the arts challenge or reflect society?

What you're going to learn:

- Key terms and expressions associated with the arts
- What artistic styles are and how they can develop
- The nature of creativity and innovation
- How art can challenge society

Liverpool, Capital of Culture 2008

In 2008 Liverpool was European capital of culture. The purpose of the 'capital of culture' is so that the designated city can showcase the arts and its own cultural development. Using EU subsidies, European capitals of culture have transformed their cultural base. In Liverpool a vast range of artistic activities have taken place, from music to visual arts, theatre and dance, poetry, comedy, film and TV and many festivals. A highlight was the 2008 Turner Prize competition. Being capital of culture has offered a complete picture of the arts in a single city in just one year.

'The arts' is a very broad term covering a wide range of different activities and **disciplines**. It can be interpreted in a variety of different ways and applied to a range of subjects and disciplines dealing with human creativity and social life, including each of the visual and performing arts. Ideally you should know about art (such as painting, sculpture, printmaking), architecture, film, music, dance, literature (including novels, poetry and plays) and drama (theatre). You could even add cookery, gardening, knitting and sewing (embroidery). Each of these activities requires creativity.

The range of 'the arts' is so vast that no one individual could ever be expected to know everything about all of them. This chapter gives you the opportunity to focus on activities that really interest you. You should select one or two of these different disciplines to study. Artistic activity, in all of its different forms, can be found throughout history. You can concentrate on things that are being done today, but it is more interesting to compare and contrast artistic activity today with examples taken from earlier ages. In this chapter there are examples of the sort of things you need to know about, but there is plenty of opportunity for you to research your own areas of interest.

Key terms

discipline – a defined body of knowledge

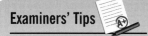

The development of artistic style

Many artists deny that there are different artistic **styles** since each work of art is unique. However, it is helpful to use the idea of style to classify or categorise different works or artists according to similar shared characteristics. Classification makes it easier to put works of art into historical, social or artistic contexts. A work can be categorised as belonging to a particular style by considering the artistic content, the period when it was produced and the techniques used by the artist. Each 'style' has a descriptive title.

Unfortunately some labels are confusing since they mean different things in different art forms. 'Classical' when applied to music is a general term for music written between c.1600 and the present day, but it also refers specifically to a type of music written between about 1750 and 1790. However, classical architecture includes the buildings of ancient Rome and Greece, features copied from the ancient world in the Renaissance period (15th and 16th centuries) and, in Britain, in the 17th and 18th centuries.

When trying to classify a piece of art, some criteria appear useful, but are not helpful. The price paid for a piece of art, or where it is kept, won't help you to classify work in a particular style. However, they may help if you want to know how important or valuable a work is thought to be today. You will not be expected to know everything about all different styles, but you should have a good knowledge of the main characteristics of at least two different styles and be able to identify and write about one or two artists and one or two works associated with a style.

To give an example, music classified as Baroque will usually share these characteristics:

- composed c.1600–c.1750
- has a sense of movement, tension and energy using ornamental notes
- includes strong contrasts of 'light' and 'shade'
- closely follows strict stylistic 'rules'
- expresses emotions and encourages them in the listener
- each piece focuses on a single theme and/or emotion
- performers are expected to improvise on composer's ideas
- generally composed for patrons and chamber performance
- includes a bass 'continuo' (usually harpsichord or cello).

Leading Baroque composers and works include Bach, e.g. *The Well Tempered Clavier* (solo keyboard); Handel, e.g. *Messiah* (oratorio); Monteverdi, e.g. *Orfeo* (opera); and Vivaldi, e.g. *The Four Seasons* (violin concerto).

Influences on artistic styles

As well as the characteristics of different styles, you need to know about factors that influenced the development of a new style. Influences will vary in significance according to the times. Influences you should consider include:

- economic conditions
- political circumstances (influences, demand, restriction)
- social conditions and groups
- fashion and popular taste
- key events (war, catastrophe, revolution)
- new attitudes in society
- availability of new or different materials or technology.

For example, why did the Renaissance develop? There was no single cause, but factors included:

- new attitudes to cultural and intellectual life
- revived interest in the art and teaching of the ancient world
- political and cultural changes after the fall of Constantinople (1453)
- ability to spread new ideas thanks to printing and trade
- a spirit of enquiry and willingness to challenge traditions
- new materials and equipment (such as oil paints and canvas)
- a greater interest in realism and perspective
- humanistic methods of study and a new interest in science and human anatomy
- patrons willing to accept and pay for new styles of work
- increased wealth to invest in the arts.

One of the most important factors is the originality of the artist, writer or composer. Renaissance art was influenced by great talents such as Botticelli, Brunelleschi, Giotto, Leonardo da Vinci, Michelangelo and Titian. Genuinely new styles are often linked to an individual who saw a new way to do things. If new ideas or methods prove popular, they may be adopted by others. Eventually a new style will emerge and be defined.

Literature, the most difficult art form to classify stylistically, is most easily classified by period (when it was written), genre (the type of literature it is) or thematic approach (such as romantic, war, horror, science-fiction).

When you have decided on the artistic form to study, you need to identify two or more different styles. Research and list key characteristics of each style. (A key characteristic is what gives a style its identity and allows it to be differentiated from other styles.) It is probably easiest to do this by concentrating on individual artists, musicians or writers who are associated with your chosen style. Comparing the lists will enable you to distinguish between the two. In visual art a good comparison is between Impressionist painters (such as Monet or Degas) and Pop Artists (such as Lichtenstein or Warhol). In music a good comparison is between older styles of music (such as composers like Handel, Mozart or Tchaikovsky) and recent forms (such as Garage, Hip Hop or Punk).

Taking it further

Research the work of artists who helped to develop new artistic styles. You could consider: Monet (painting); Stockhausen (music); Beckett (drama); Lang (cinema); Gaudí (architecture). How and why were they innovative?

Key terms

Some important styles associated with most disciplines are Gothic (1100–1400); Renaissance (1400–1700); Baroque (1600–1750); Rococo (1720–1750); Classical (1750–1790); Romantic (1780–1900); Impressionism (1880–1920); Modern (1900–1950); Post-Modern (after 1950).

Examiners' Tips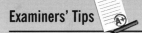

Remember that **you** choose the artistic styles to study and write about. It is important that, whatever your chosen style(s), you have knowledge and understanding of different works and different artists.

Creativity and innovation

When you write a letter, doodle, plant flowers or sing you are being creative. It is too easy to think that **creativity** is something only specially gifted people have. It is a universal quality that marks human beings out as unique. It is not a measure of great quality or skill.

Creativity is usually associated with the arts. Some of the arts, such as painting, music, dance or sculpture, are described as 'creative arts'. Each of these areas produces new work which would not have existed without the artists' efforts. This is what creativity is all about. A painter turns a blank canvas into a painting; a writer or composer converts words and sounds into books or music; a sculptor shapes stone or metal into a statue or abstract figure. The same is true in architecture, drama, dance or any other creative art. They involve acts of creation based on an **artist's** effort, skill and imagination.

Creativity is all around us. Mills and Boon romances are the result of creativity. They may not have the originality, insight into human emotions or lasting qualities of Shakespeare or Dickens, but they are creative. Similarly, a park or a garden shows creativity, even though lacking the originality of vision of Humphry Repton, 'Capability' Brown or even Alan Titchmarsh. A funny birthday card or the latest pop song are just as much examples of creativity as a painting by Raphael or a Lennon and McCartney song.

Staying power

Some works of art possess qualities which set them apart. This type of art has longevity, and will be popular for many years. It is often described as a good or outstanding example of a particular style or art form. Art critics will identify its distinctive qualities and characteristics.

By contrast, most works of art survive only for short periods of time and have little lasting effect on audiences. This can be illustrated with music, but is equally true of other art forms. The Rock 'n' Roll revolution of the 1950s and 1960s produced hundreds if not thousands of pieces of music and innumerable singers. Most of these are long forgotten, except by those people who first listened to them. Today people have heard of Elvis Presley, Cliff Richard, The Beatles or the Rolling Stones, but few have heard of The Applejacks. Similarly, 'Yesterday', 'My Way' or 'Heartbreak Hotel' are remembered and played today, but who remembers Mark Wynter's 'In Your Heart'?

Art works survive for many different reasons. They are not necessarily 'better' than works which are forgotten or disappear. Luck or the influence of individuals is undoubtedly significant. Some works have characteristics which appeal to many generations but others only relate to specific times and circumstances. Some works of art do possess qualities which set them apart as superior to others. These qualities may concern content or **form** or the level of skill demonstrated by an artist or performer.

Key terms

creativity – the application of imagination and skill to bring into existence something which did not previously exist

artist – can refer to a painter but it is also a general word applied to anyone who practises or performs in any of the artistic forms

form – the visible shape of a work as distinct from the content

Activity

1. Discuss whether commercial pressures are more important than genuine originality in bringing about changes in artistic style.
2. What circumstances may (a) encourage and (b) discourage innovation in the arts?

Taking it further

Choose any art form and identify five contemporary works which you feel will survive and be regarded by future generations as 'good art'. List the qualities of each work that will help them to survive. Now list five works of art which you believe will not retain lasting popularity. What qualities do they lack?

Innovation in the arts

Some works of art or artists are innovative since they possess qualities that make them unique or original. These qualities may influence the establishment or contribute to the development of new artistic styles. To do this the innovative quality must impress other artists or audiences and make them want to copy or build on the innovation. New ideas or techniques will be adopted generally only if they have a broad appeal. Many **innovations** have not been pursued because they have failed to make significant impact.

Musical instruments offer good examples of innovations that failed to have a lasting impact. Over the centuries many different instruments have been invented as composers have sought specific sounds. Some new instruments like the saxophone have become very popular, but others like the chalumeau (similar to a recorder or clarinet) or the arpeggione (like a cello) lacked the necessary qualities to survive and become accepted.

Each of the arts has numerous examples of innovations that have brought about significant change. In architecture important technical innovations which changed the style of buildings for ever were the counter-weighted tower crane and the safety elevator (lift). In the 15th century Brunelleschi's counter-weighted tower crane allowed architects to design and build vast domes. In 1853 Otis's safety lift played a key part in allowing architects to create skyscrapers. Every urban skyline shows the importance of both of these inventions.

Oil-based paints were a significant technical innovation in painting. Coming into general use about 1410, these slow-drying paints gave artists time to build up their work. It was a major contribution to the development of realistic painting.

Artists who did things differently often experienced criticism and opposition from the establishment. In the 1870s Impressionism, Monet's new style of painting, met with great hostility. He and his followers rejected the popular realistic style of other artists and used new painting techniques. In the early 20th century, however, Impressionism was accepted and influenced the development of many later styles. It encouraged artists to challenge traditional methods and established practices.

Pop Art developed in the 1960s and showed the impact of innovative artists such as Andy Warhol, who used new materials to paint in a new style. A good starting point to study innovation in the arts is recent Man Booker or Turner Prize winners. The Man Booker Prize is awarded annually for the best original full-length novel written in the English language, and the Turner Prize is awarded each year to a British artist under 50. The Turner Prize is associated with conceptual art but it can be awarded to an artist working in any style or tradition. Artists who are shortlisted usually work in 'innovative' media, such as video art, installation art or unconventional sculpture.

Key terms

innovation – a change in something already existing or the introduction of something new. In the arts it refers to the development of new methods, techniques, materials or ideas. The essential feature of innovation is that artists do something never done previously.

Taking it further

Select an artist whose originality introduced significant change. What did they do that was innovative and how did it influence the work of others? Investigate the significance of the works they produced.

Activity

Investigate which recent works were nominated for either the Turner or the Man Booker prizes. What were their distinctive characteristics and how did the judges justify their decisions?

Examiners' Tips

Many examiners will have limited knowledge of very recent music. If you answer general questions about style, use your own knowledge and experience of popular music to create a convincing impression.

Chapter 9 Summary

By now, you should have knowledge and understanding of:

1 Key terms and expressions associated with the arts

- What 'art', 'artist' and 'the arts' mean and the distinctions between them.
- What the main artistic forms are (including painting; music; literature and architecture).

2 What artistic styles are and how they can develop

- How different artistic styles have developed and the different influences on artists.
- How and why works of art can be classified; what criteria might be used to help with classification.
- Why artistic styles change; who or what can bring about change; whether the changes are real or merely superficial.
- Key features of at least two different artistic styles.

3 The nature of creativity and innovation

- What creativity and innovation mean and the difference between them.
- Innovative artists and works of art and some of their key innovative features.
- The difference between genuine innovation and works that are made to appear 'different' but which do not really introduce anything new.
- The challenge and problems associated with the interpretation of different works of art.

4 How art can challenge society

- How to answer 'What is the purpose of art?' with evidence drawn from the fields of art you have studied.
- The extent to which art is a reflection of the society that existed when it was created; whether artists are more concerned to describe life 'as it is' or whether their aim is to show it 'as it should be'.
- Ways in which art can challenge society and make people question values and beliefs, with examples of artists or artistic works that have challenged society in some way.

Chapter 10 Is the UK really a democracy?

What you're going to learn:

- The UK political parties, their key policies, levels of internal democracy and the differences between them
- The membership, funding, campaigning and recent successes of UK political parties
- The electoral systems in the UK, possible reforms and voting behaviour
- The ways in which individuals and groups contribute to the political process
- The role of the UK in the world, including membership of and participation in the Commonwealth, EU, NATO and UN
- The significance of international activities and the extent of democratic control by UK citizens in foreign policy matters.

In a democracy, the will of the majority prevails while the interests of minorities must always be respected. All males over the age of 21, and women aged over 30, were given the right to vote in 1918; in 1928 the law was changed to allow women over the age of 21 the right to vote. The voting age was lowered to 18 in 1969 and in 2008 there is an on-going campaign to reduce this to 16.

People are usually asked to vote for candidates or parties. With about 75,000 potential voters in most constituencies, candidates usually have little chance of success unless they are backed by a political party. The party's members can go out and campaign for votes and deliver leaflets during the election.

In the 1950s just two parties – Labour and Conservative – contested most areas. They gained 95% of all votes cast and almost all MPs elected were either Labour or Conservative. Many people now support other parties.

There are calls for referendums to be held to decide issues where it is thought parties fail to fully reflect public opinion. There have also been strong complaints about the reliability of the traditional 'first past the post' voting system presently used in UK general elections.

Activity

What similarities and differences do you notice in the two general election results shown here for Ludlow (Shropshire) in 1955 and 2005?

LUDLOW 1955	
Electorate:	47,040
Turnout:	33,753 (71.8%)
Conservative	20,816 (61.7%)
Labour	12,937 (38.3%)
Majority	7,879 (23.4%)

LUDLOW 2005	
Electorate:	64,572
Turnout:	46,540 (72.1%)
Conservative	20,929 (45.1%)
Lib Dem	18,952 (40.7%)
Labour	4,974 (10.7%)
Green	852 (1.8%)
UKIP	783 (1.7%)
Majority	2,027 (4.4%)

Taking it further

Now find out about the election results where you live or where your school or college is located.
1. What proportion of people actually voted?
2. How many candidates were there?
3. What share of the electorate's support did the winning candidate receive?

Political parties in the UK

A political party is a group of people (and sometimes organisations) with shared ideological or policy aims seeking to achieve power through contesting elections. They are unlike pressure groups, which may have the same aims but which do not normally contest elections.

	House of Commons	House of Lords	Scottish Parliament	Welsh Assembly	Northern Ireland Assembly	European Parliament
Labour	352	216	46	26	0	19
Conservative	194	202	16	12	0	27
Liberal Democrat	63	78	16	6	7	12
Green Party	0	1	2	0	1	2
UKIP	0	2	0	0	0	12
Plaid Cymru	3	0	0	15	0	1
Scottish National Party	6	0	47	0	0	2
Democratic Unionist	9	0	0	0	36	1
Ulster Unionist	1	0	0	0	18	1
SDLP	3	0	0	0	16	0
Sinn Fein	5	0	0	0	28	1
Respect	1	0	0	0	0	0
Independent	5	232	1	1	2	0
Speaker and Deputies	4	1	1	0	0	0
Total number of members	**646**	**732**	**129**	**60**	**108**	**UK=78**

The memberships of UK and EU parliaments and assemblies, January 2008

- All MPs in the *House of Commons* are elected in single member constituencies using the first past the post method of election. SDLP is the Social Democratic and Labour Party which puts forward candidates in Northern Ireland only. The Sinn Fein MPs have not sworn an Oath of Allegiance and taken their seats, so they cannot take part in debates or vote. Mr Speaker (acts as a neutral Chairman of debates) and his deputies in the House of Commons do not normally vote The number of MPs will rise to 650 after the next general election as a result of boundary changes.
- In the *House of Lords* there are 615 life peers and 91 hereditary peers. The independent peers listed above include 181 crossbench (non-party) peers, 1 Labour independent, 1 Conservative independent, 26 bishops and archbishops and 23 judges. The total membership of 732 excludes 16 peers who have been given permission to be absent for health or other reasons.
- The *Scottish Parliament* comprises 73 MSPs elected in constituencies and 56 via regional lists using the Additional Member System.
- The *Welsh Assembly* comprises 40 AMs elected in constituencies and 20 via regional lists using the Additional Member System.
- Members of the *Northern Ireland Assembly* are elected in 18 six-member constituencies using the single transferable vote (STV) system. The seven members indicated in the Liberal Democrat column are members of the Alliance Party, which is aligned to the Liberal Democrats. One of the two independent members is a Progressive Unionist.
- The UK elects 75 members (of a total 732 members) to the *European Parliament* using a regional list system based on 12 multi-member constituencies in England, Scotland and Wales, and three further members are elected from Northern Ireland using the STV method.

Taking it further

Look at the websites for the different political assemblies and make sure you understand the differences between the systems of election used for each of them.

Why are the party representations so different in the different elected bodies?

- *Timing* is a big factor: the European Parliament election was held in 2004, the Westminster election in 2005, and elections to the devolved bodies were held in 2007.
- The public *change their mind* between elections. Some analysts believe they change much more now than before because people's partisan identification (strength of commitment to a particular party) is now much weaker than in the past.
- Different *voting systems* are in use: the Greens and UKIP have not been able to win a constituency seat in the House of Commons using a first past the post election system, but they have met with more success when a system of proportional representation is used.
- *Personalities* are important too. At the time of the 2005 general election, the leaders of the three main parties were Tony Blair (Labour), Michael Howard (Conservative) and Charles Kennedy (Liberal Democrat); by January 2008 Sir Menzies Campbell had come and gone as Lib Dem Leader, and the three parties were led, respectively, by Gordon Brown, David Cameron and Nick Clegg.

Key features of political parties

There were just two parties in most constituency contests in the 1950s – Labour and Conservative. Today four, five or six candidates is typical, as the results in Ludlow showed (see page 91). All the main parties play an active part in local government. For example, Labour controls Gateshead and Manchester, the Conservatives control Swindon and Lincoln, and the Lib Dems are in charge in Eastleigh and St Albans.

Political parties sometimes seem remote from voters, saying what the focus groups suggest we want to hear rather than what they truly stand for. All parties claim to give their members a big say but often it is the leaders whose wishes prevail. Perhaps this is partly why party membership figures have fallen sharply in the past ten years.

The old division of 'Conservatives right wing, Labour left wing' means little these days. However, Conservatives do still favour smaller government than Labour, preferring to leave more things to individuals, charities, voluntary organisations and businesses rather than the state. Often parties seem to be claiming to be better managers rather than to have better policy goals.

Sometimes people do vote positively for a particular party. For example, many Asian voters supported the Lib Dems in 2005 because of their opposition to the Iraq war; also, many university students liked their opposition to tuition fees, which brought the Lib Dems gains in university towns such as Cambridge, Bristol, Manchester and Leeds. Often people vote tactically for the party which they think has the best chance of defeating the party they like least. The Conservatives have lost out badly in Scotland and the North of England through tactical voting. In 1955 they had 23 MPs in Birmingham, Manchester, Sheffield, Liverpool and Glasgow; but in 2008 they had none.

Party campaigning and funding is monitored by the Electoral Commission, which can question whether donations to a party are lawful. Some people want state funding for political parties. They say it keeps democracy healthy if there is less dependence on trade unions, big business or wealthy individuals, who may then expect favours and influence in return.

Activity

Find out which party controls the council where you live and what changes took place at the last set of elections. Do you think local people voted according to national party labels or because of genuinely local issues?

Taking it further

Keep an eye open for any elections which occur during your course of study. Often big swings between political parties occur in the May local elections, or there are by-elections to fill a vacancy if an MP dies or retires.

Activity

Have a look at the Electoral Commission website and see what matters they have recently been investigating or on which they have reported.

UK electoral systems

The first past the post voting system, used in general elections, is easy to use and count. It is familiar and has produced clear-cut election results (i.e. avoiding coalition or minority governments) in most elections for at least a century and a half. However, proportional voting systems are used in elections for the European Parliament and the devolved bodies. Critics have pointed out weaknesses in the first past the post system:

1. It may allow someone to become an MP with very little support from the electorate. In 2005 in Brighton Pavilion, the electorate was 68,087 but only 15,427 (22.6%) voted for the successful Labour MP, David Lepper.
2. Sometimes the first past the post system gives the biggest number of seats in Parliament to the party which came second in terms of total number of votes, for example in the general elections of 1951 and February 1974.
3. Often the result for an area will be badly distorted. In 2007 the votes cast in the six constituencies in Cumbria were Conservatives 92,367 (38.2%), Labour 83,720 (34.6%) and Liberal Democrats 56,452 (23.3%). Perhaps you might expect the Conservatives to win 3 of the seats, Labour 2 and the Lib Dems 1; in reality the result was Conservative 1, Labour 4, Lib Dem 1.
4. In 2007, Labour won 35.3% of the national vote but were rewarded with 55% of the seats in Parliament. They had more votes than any other party (so were the largest minority) but not more votes than all the other parties put together, so should they have had an overall majority in terms of seats?

Different voting systems

Proportional representation (PR) means that seats are allocated in the same proportion as votes cast. If a party secured an overall majority of votes, PR would give the party an overall majority of seats. What it won't do is give a party a big majority of seats if it doesn't have a big majority of votes.

Electoral reform would occur if a majority of MPs voted to make a change. So if there was a 'hung' Parliament, for example, and Labour or Conservative needed Lib Dem support to command a majority in the House of Commons, then the price to be paid might well be a different voting system.

Voting behaviour

Voting behaviour is complex and can be affected by these factors:

- *Turnout* Many people don't bother to vote unless a particular issue captures their interest. Election contests are most intense in marginal seats where there is a real possibility that the seat will change parties. Tactical voting is often an important factor, with the 'third' party being squeezed, for example in Durham in 2005 where the Conservative vote almost halved.
- *Issues* Particular issues can have a big effect. In the 1980s Conservatives gained support from council house tenants who wanted to buy their homes. In 2005 many voters liked the Lib Dems' opposition to the council tax, while the Iraq war proved very unpopular among Labour voters.
- *Partisan alignment* This has a strong link to class. In the 1950s people were often strongly committed to a particular class and party: the working class voted Labour, the middle class Conservative. Such identifications are much weaker now (only 16% now admit to strong identification); there can sometimes be big swings in elections as people change their minds depending on the issue which concerns them most. In 2005 Labour's former

working-class supporters were willing to vote for a range of different parties. Among professional and managerial former Conservative voters there was a strong movement to both Labour and the Lib Dems.

- *Age* Only 45% of the 18–24 age group voted in 2005 compared with over 80% of the 55+ age groups. It used to be said that older people were more likely to vote Conservative, but this tendency seems to have been replaced by a more self-interested approach in which people vote for the party they identify as best safeguarding their economic interests.
- *Education* For the past 20 years there seems to have been an increasing tendency for people with a university education to be the most likely to support 'third' parties such as Greens or Lib Dems.
- *Gender* A focus on family issues and the welfare of children was probably the reason why women favoured Labour in 2005, while men were more evenly divided between the parties.
- *Geography* In 2005 the Conservatives were strongest in East and South East regions and weakest in Scotland; the Lib Dems were strongest in the South West and Scotland; while Labour strength was in Wales, Yorkshire and Humberside, North East and North West England and Scotland. In many northern urban areas, the main battle was between Labour and the Lib Dems; in many rural areas between Conservatives and Lib Dems. Different two-party systems seemed to be emerging in different parts of the country.

The power of pressure groups

Pressure groups are an important part of our democracy. They provide a means by which individuals can campaign to change government policy on a particular matter. If it is proposed to close a hospital or school, they can organise opposition which will often prove successful. As memberships of political parties have gone down, so memberships of pressure groups have increased, suggesting that most people know the particular issues which matter to them and on which they want to make a difference. Pressure groups are often categorised into *insider* and *outsider* groups.

An *insider* group such as the National Farmers Union, Age Concern or the Child Poverty Action Group will have good relations with the government, which may depend on the group for technical information and advice. Such groups do not engage in noisy protests because the government will welcome their inputs into policy making and usually take account of the points they suggest.

By contrast, governments will be largely indifferent if not hostile to the views of an *outsider* group, which could be protesting about ID cards or the Iraq war or campaigning for other changes in government policy. Groups such as Liberty may be able to brief an MP or member of the House of Lords to ask questions, speak on their behalf in Parliament or perhaps put forward a private member's bill, but the chances of changing anything by such routes are slim and the way they are most likely to achieve their goals is by articles in the press, publicising their blogs and getting on radio or television, so that the government may feel the need to move in the direction of the group to avoid defeat at the next election.

Taking it further

Go to the Parliament website, www.parliament.uk, and see what private members' bills are in the pipeline. See if you can work out which pressure groups are supporting the MP or peer. Follow up by reading the report of any debate in Hansard.

The UK's role in the world 2: International activities and democratic control

The reputation and standing of the UK in the world depends not so much on the organisations to which we belong but how we use the platforms that such memberships provide. In part our reputation will be dictated by history and the length of people's memories; here many interpretations are inevitable. In the 20th century:

- Did the British Empire bring many more benefits than problems to our colonies? Or did we exploit their natural resources for our own ends?
- Were we justified in challenging Hitler's megalomania?
- Should we have intervened more actively in post-Tito Yugloslavia to halt the civil war in the Balkans?
- Did we ever decide whether our principal loyalties were with Europe or across the Atlantic with the USA and Canada?

Britain's role in the world today

Britain's role in the world can be defined by factors such as:

- *How we use our memberships of international bodies in an increasingly global environment* For example, progress was stalled in 2008 in the World Trade Organisation programme to cut tariffs and develop world trade to the benefit of the poorest countries in the world. The Doha round of negotiations was a big disappointment: could the UK have done more to persuade others to squeeze an agreement out of the negotiations?
- *The determination we demonstrate to get the whole world to respond to the problems of global warming and climate change* At Bali (2008) world leaders were unable to agree truly tangible progress to challenge the problems of global warming, could Britain have done more?
- *The skill with which we communicate our view of the world to people in many other countries* Many would say that the BBC World Service does a brilliant job in earning Britain much respect and raising its profile.
- *The strength and durability of our commitment to scholarship*.
- *Our commitment to research and development*.
- *The volume of our imports and exports and the extent to which we are willing to give access on favourable terms to developing countries*. One good development in recent years has been the growth and support of Fair Trade programmes.
- *The nature and extent of aid to other countries and how far such aid is offered without strings* This includes provision of education and medicines to combat the spread of AIDS and debt relief to wipe out the burdens of past borrowing. In 2006/7 the UK spent £7,487 million, including large amounts of debt relief. Excluding debt relief, aid spending increased by 9% between 2005/6 and 2006/7, with India, Tanzania, Sudan and Bangladesh receiving the lion's share.

Taking it further

What progress has been made on world trade and climate change since this chapter was written?

Activity

What other criteria can you and your friends think of to determine how the UK is viewed around the world?

How democratic is UK foreign policy?

The only international organisation to which the UK belongs which has direct democratic input by the British people is the European Union.

- The UK has 78 of the 732 members of the European Parliament, although in some senses this is more of a scrutiny body than a parliament.
- The UK's 78 members sit in party groups. For example, of those elected in 2004 the 19 Labour members sit in the Socialist group of 215 MEPs and the 12 Liberal Democrats sit in the European Liberals and Reform group of 103 MEPs. The UK Conservatives have discussed switching to become part of a new grouping after 2009.
- Most legislation for the EU comes from the Council of Ministers. Here a member of the UK government will take part in discussions about making new law; if the law is to be about finance, it will probably be the Chancellor of the Exchequer who attends; if it is an environmental matter then the Secretary of State for Environment, Food and Rural Affairs (DEFRA) will be the relevant minister.

Since 1945, when the United Nations was formed, there has been a United Nations Association in the UK with branches throughout the country. A typical example of such support came in January 2008 when, with input from United Nations Association-UK, Martin Caton MP put forward a new Early Day Motion (EDM) in the House of Commons calling for a comprehensive ban on cluster munitions. UNA-UK members were asked to urge their MPs to support the motion. Within three weeks 62 MPs from all parties had backed the motion.

The UK doesn't elect people to go to NATO or Commonwealth meetings, but that does not mean there isn't a strong democratic framework in place here. When the Foreign Secretary goes to a Commonwealth meeting or the Secretary of State for Defence to a NATO meeting, they report back on the event to the House of Commons, and either or both of them are likely to be summoned to a Select Committee to respond to detailed questioning. MPs on such committees tend to have expert knowledge of such policy areas; the committees subsequently issue reports which are publicly available.

Do UK citizens have sufficient say over foreign policy? It is undoubtedly true that information can be readily obtained, and the government's role in its overseas work is accountable and open to scrutiny from MPs and MEPs. However, on the most significant foreign policy in recent years, no amount of protesting would deter the UK government from joining in the war in Iraq, which in 2008 is unpopular. The trouble is that retrospection doesn't work well; according to polling, the war was more popular when we launched it in 2003 (and when Parliament voted for it) than it is now.

Chapter 10 Summary

By now, you should have knowledge and understanding of:

1 The UK political parties, their key policies, levels of internal democracy and the differences between them

- Levels of party support at Westminster, in the devolved bodies and in the European Parliament.
- The reasons why and the extent to which party strengths differ in the various assemblies.
- The changing nature of the UK party system as more parties emerge.

2 The membership, funding, campaigning and recent successes of UK political parties

- The apparent decline of ideology and diminishing party memberships.
- The changing geography of the political landscape.
- The increased role of the Electoral Commission.

3 The electoral systems in the UK, possible reforms and voting behaviour

- The strengths and weaknesses of the first past the post system.
- An awareness of other systems now in use in the UK and an assessment of their impact.
- The extent of and reasons for increased volatility on the part of UK voters.

4 The ways in which individuals and groups contribute to the political process

- The significance of issues that lead to changed voting behaviour.
- The significance of factors such as geography, age, turnout and class in explaining voting behaviour.
- The significance of pressure groups.

5 The role of the UK in the world, including membership of and participation in the Commonwealth, EU, NATO and UN

- Our role as a member of the Security Council of the United Nations.
- The importance of international organisations in an increasingly global environment.
- The significance of the European Union.
- Continuing relationships with NATO and the Commonwealth.

6 The significance of international activities and the extent of democratic control by UK citizens in foreign policy matters

- How the UK's reputation and standing in the world is to be judged.
- How important are trade and aid, and which is the better strategy to help poor countries.
- Whether foreign policy is conducted within a strong enough framework of democratic control.

Multiple choice questions

Here are some examples of multiple choice questions as used in Section A of Unit 2 of the exam. In the exam there will be 20 questions.

Choose an answer A, B, C, or D and put a cross in the box (X).
If you change your mind, put a line through the box (✖) and then mark your new answer with a cross (X).

1. An example of a subculture would be

    ☒ **A**   a queue at the sales

    ☒ **B**   passengers on a bus

    ☒ **C**   people who buy raffle tickets

    ☒ **D**   teenage gangs

    (Total 1 mark)

2. Which one of the following 'evils' was among those that the welfare state was planned to eliminate?

    ☒ **A**   dishonesty

    ☒ **B**   ignorance

    ☒ **C**   immorality

    ☒ **D**   inequality

    (Total 1 mark)

3.
> The type of people we are, and the way we behave towards others, is a direct result of the way we are brought up. We learn the values that society regards as important in our early years at home and at school. Our biology may be the main influence on the colour of our hair and the shape of our feet, but even these are not fixed for ever. We are what we are made to be and not what we are born as.

This passage is dealing with aspects of

    ☒ **A**   behavioural therapy

    ☒ **B**   environmental reductionism

    ☒ **C**   the nature–nurture debate

    ☒ **D**   value consensus

    (Total 1 mark)

4. Which of the following best describes the statement 'We are what we are made to be'?

   ⊠ **A** belief

   ⊠ **B** error

   ⊠ **C** fact

   ⊠ **D** science

(Total 1 mark)

5. Individuals learn the attitudes and values of society and their role within it through a process of

   ⊠ **A** identification

   ⊠ **B** secularisation

   ⊠ **C** socialisation

   ⊠ **D** socialism

(Total 1 mark)

6. Which of the following might lead to increased unemployment?

   ⊠ **A** the country becomes involved in military conflict

   ⊠ **B** the government introduces a new tax on employment

   ⊠ **C** the retirement age for men and women is raised to 70

   ⊠ **D** a good summer leading to bumper harvests

(Total 1 mark)

7. A nuclear family is

   ⊠ **A** one in which the parents are not married

   ⊠ **B** one in which there are no children

   ⊠ **C** one in which there are only parents and dependent children

   ⊠ **D** one in which three or more generations live together

(Total 1 mark)

8. Which of these definitions is **not** a true meaning of the term 'culture'?

   ⊠ **A** the arts and other examples of human achievement

   ⊠ **B** the customs and institutions of a particular group or nation

   ⊠ **C** the process of growing living plants or organisms

   ⊠ **D** a system or variety of religious worship and belief

(Total 1 mark)

9. Which of the following laws does **not** concern equality of opportunity?

    ☒ **A** Disability Discrimination Act

    ☒ **B** Divorce Reform Act

    ☒ **C** Gender Recognition Act

    ☒ **D** Race Relations Act

    (Total 1 mark)

10. Which of the following phrases completes this sentence: 'If they want to increase market share, editors of mass circulation newspapers will ...'?

    ☒ **A** only print stories if they are paid to do so

    ☒ **B** print more stories about the private lives of celebrities

    ☒ **C** reduce human interest stories and increase political analysis

    ☒ **D** increase the price charged to customers

    (Total 1 mark)

11. Which of the following phrases completes this sentence: 'The mass media are ...'?

    ☒ **A** a means of communication with large audiences

    ☒ **B** not dependent on modern technology

    ☒ **C** set up by people who want to serve humanity

    ☒ **D** generally considered to have little influence on people

    (Total 1 mark)

12. Which of these laws does **not** limit what newspapers can print?

    ☒ **A** the Equal Opportunities Act

    ☒ **B** the laws of libel

    ☒ **C** the Obscene Publications Act

    ☒ **D** the Official Secrets Act

    (Total 1 mark)

13. Which one of the following is an example of a 'quality' newspaper?

    ☒ **A** Daily Mirror

    ☒ **B** News of the World

    ☒ **C** The Sun

    ☒ **D** The Times

    (Total 1 mark)

14. Which one of the following organisations regulates the media in the UK?

☒ **A** Ofcom

☒ **B** Ofgen

☒ **C** Ofsted

☒ **D** Ofwat

(Total 1 mark)

15. The term genre means

☒ **A** the materials used by an artist

☒ **B** a particular style of art

☒ **C** art created in or near Genoa in Italy

☒ **D** the unique skill of an artist

(Total 1 mark)

16. Which of these factors would be most likely to restrict the development of an existing artistic style?

☒ **A** availability of new materials

☒ **B** interest in new fashions

☒ **C** religious or political opposition

☒ **D** increasing prosperity

(Total 1 mark)

17. The Man Booker prize is a competition for

☒ **A** architects

☒ **B** musicians

☒ **C** painters

☒ **D** writers

(Total 1 mark)

18. If the takings at an exhibition over five weeks are: Week 1: £2,000, Week 2: £2,000, Week 3: £3,000, Week 4: £6,000, Week 5: £7,000, what is the mean for weekly takings?

☒ **A** £2,000

☒ **B** £3,000

☒ **C** £4,000

☒ **D** £5,000

(Total 1 mark)

19. If the takings at an exhibition over five weeks are Week 1: £2,000,
Week 2: £2,000, Week 3: £3,000, Week 4: £6,000, Week 5: £7,000,
what is the median for weekly takings?

    ☒ **A** £2,000

    ☒ **B** £3,000

    ☒ **C** £6,000

    ☒ **D** £7,000

(Total 1 mark)

20. Which one of the following countries is a member of the European Union?

    ☒ **A** Greenland

    ☒ **B** Iceland

    ☒ **C** Norway

    ☒ **D** Poland

(Total 1 mark)

21. To which of the bodies listed below are representatives directly elected by
UK citizens?

    ☒ **A** Commonwealth of Nations

    ☒ **B** European Parliament

    ☒ **C** North Atlantic Treaty Organisation

    ☒ **D** United Nations Organisation

(Total 1 mark)

22. Which of these statements about a parliamentary constituency is correct?
It is an area that elects

    ☒ **A** a Justice of the Peace (JP)

    ☒ **B** a mayor

    ☒ **C** an MP

    ☒ **D** a town councillor

(Total 1 mark)

23. Which of the following forms of voting is used to elect members of the
British parliament?

    ☒ **A** alternative

    ☒ **B** first past the post

    ☒ **C** preferential

    ☒ **D** proportional

(Total 1 mark)

Exam technique

Top tips

Examiners' Tips

In the exam look carefully at each question to see which objective is being tested and make sure that you gear your answer to satisfy its demands.

Examiners' Tips

Find out about different types of question by looking at past papers (including those for the old General Studies Specification). Your centre can provide you with these, or they are available from www.edexcel. org.uk Examiners' reports give a clear idea of how to approach each type of question.

Examiners' Tips

Look at news, comment or feature sections of quality newspapers or magazines to develop your knowledge and understanding of important issues. They will show you the importance of different perspectives and viewpoints. You will also be able to apply your thinking and analytical skills in a live environment.

General Studies is not simply a test of general knowledge. To do well you must prepare for all aspects of the exam. Don't just rely on natural ability. Other subjects rely on specific disciplines and clearly defined specialist knowledge. In General Studies you must draw on a broad knowledge and understanding of various disciplines and apply the skills and techniques associated with them. Good preparation takes time and effort and should not be left to the last minute. These tips can help you prepare.

1. Know the Specification. The Specification contains all the essential information you need for the exam. It outlines the areas of knowledge you need and expands on it in an appendix. This is the basis of this text book. To do well you must know what is expected of you. If you have not been given a copy of the key parts of the Specification by your centre you can download a copy from www.edexcel.org.uk

2. Assessment objectives. There are four assessment objectives, given in the Specification (see page 114), which are tested in both units of the AS examination. You must demonstrate your ability in each objective. The Specification shows how different questions will be used in assessment. Some questions are geared to a single objective, but others will test two or more. Questions involving extended writing will also test communication skills (AO4).

3. Types of question. The exam consists of different types of question. Section A consists entirely of multiple choice questions; Section B contains short answer questions and extended writing questions based on data response; and Section C contains extended writing based on stimulus material. Learn to recognise each type of question and the style of answer required.

4. The structure of the exam papers. Be familiar with the structure of the papers and know the content of each unit. Since there is no choice of question, you must answer them all. Section A tests all aspects of the content, but Sections B and C will focus on specific topics. There is no transfer of marks between questions or sections.

5. Useful resources. The text book gives you the core knowledge you need, but you can add to this and strengthen your command of the subject. As well as the knowledge and skills you developed for earlier exams such as GCSE (especially your Science and Maths work) and your other A level subjects, you can make use of your own experience of everyday life. Since General Studies concerns contemporary issues you can improve understanding by watching news and current affairs programmes or engaging in discussion with others.

6. Necessary equipment. Know the equipment that you need for the exam. Have at least one spare pen. Always have a calculator in case there are application of number questions in either unit. Have a pencil and ruler in case you need to draw a graph.

7. Thinking and analytical skills. These are a key part of General Studies. Candidates who think 'natural talent' is enough and don't learn and master these skills often struggle with these questions. There is no substitute for knowing, mastering and practising thinking and analytical skills. You should find it fairly easy to accumulate marks and will develop skills that will benefit your other studies. (See also pages 5–8.)

8. Practise. It isn't enough to know what you have to do: you must be able to do it. This means regular practice. When you know the techniques and skills you need, then get as much practice as you can in using and applying them. Do this by answering the practice questions (see pages 49–54, 101–5, 116–25, 130–37), preferably under test conditions.

9. Revision, rest and refreshment. These are the three most important rules when preparing for exams. Start revision early and be systematic. Get plenty of rest, especially the night before the exam. Make sure that you have plenty of refreshment before the exam, especially breakfast. You will need extra energy if you are to do well.

Time allocation

Each examination lasts for 90 minutes and carries 90 marks, so there is the equivalent of a minute per mark. The maximum time you can afford for Section A is 20 minutes. If you complete Section A sooner you can spend more time on higher scoring questions. Ideally you should spend almost half your time on section C, where you can gain most marks. Save the last five minutes to check your answers. Attempt every question!

A useful clue in allocating time is how many lines and marks are allocated to questions in the answer book. A question with 1 or 2 marks and 5 or 6 lines will not let you score lots of marks if you write too much. It could rob you of vital time needed for other questions.

Using the answer book

- Answers are marked online. Use dark ink and be careful that your writing is not too small to read.
- Write your answers only on the lines provided and not on 'blank pages'.
- Don't write in the margins or at the top or bottom of the pages. These are outside the 'clip area' that examiners can see. Parts may actually be cut off and lost forever.
- If you cross an answer out or write part of an answer in a different part of the answer book, show clearly in the answer space where examiners can find your answer.

Examiners' terms

- Words used in questions are chosen to help you. You must read questions carefully and note the little qualifying words (such as 'one' or 'not'). In Sections B and C 'command' words tell you what type of answer is required.
- Some questions want simple information or description and will contain words like 'what', 'describe', 'give', 'which', 'name', 'identify'. These usually appear in short answer questions and often test AO1. They may only carry a single mark
- Some questions require a developed answer where you must show understanding as well as knowledge. Terms used include: 'why ...?', 'explain', 'illustrate your answer', 'examine', 'give x reasons', 'suggest'. These can test any of the assessment objectives and usually carry 2 or 3 marks.
- For terms used in extended writing questions see pages 126–9.

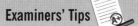

Examiners' Tips

The exam is marked online. Write in either dark blue or black ink. Faint ink and small writing are difficult to read on a computer screen. If examiners can't read your work they won't be able to give you the marks that you may deserve.

Examiners' Tips

When practising, don't always write answers out in full. Skeleton or outline answers are an excellent way to practise the application of skills and to test knowledge. They can be completed rapidly and will help you when planning extended writing in the exam.

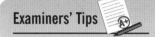

Examiners' Tips

If you find a question is very hard, don't spend too much time on it. Leave it and come back to it later.

Examiners' Tips

Some candidates draw little clocks in the margin of the exam paper to show when they should finish each section. Make sure you keep a careful eye on your watch or the clock in the exam room so that you don't run out of time.

Answering multiple choice questions

Examiners' Tips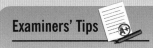

When revising, make sure you know your material as thoroughly as possible, especially the key terms.

Activity

If you want to see how other people tackle multiple choice questions look at the techniques of successful contestants on *Who Wants to Be a Millionaire?*

What are multiple choice questions?

Section A in both unit 1 and unit 2 consists of 20 multiple choice questions. Each question will carry 1 mark. These questions are an excellent way to test a broad range of material fairly quickly, but don't be misled into thinking that they are easy. They are designed to test your knowledge and to make you think carefully. There will be questions on each part of the Specification. Apart from communication (AO4) they can test any of the assessment objectives. Some questions may test the use and application of number or thinking and analytical skills. Your main advantage is that you don't have to think of your own answer since the correct answer is always given you.

There are different types of multiple choice questions, which usually follow a similar format. A stem is followed by a choice of four different answers from which you select the correct one. Sometimes they may involve finishing off a sentence, but usually they are structured as straightforward questions. They may be freestanding or based on stimulus material such as a table, graph or passage. Some questions will test your understanding of key terms or definitions, but some may expect you to analyse new information or work out answers from information that is given to you.

To succeed with multiple choice questions you must master a broad range of detailed and specific information. Don't be misled by people who tell you this type of question is easy; you may score a few marks by guessing but not enough for a good grade. However, you can get 100% of answers right (which is more than for most exam questions) provided you are properly prepared.

The traditional question format will form the majority of multiple choice questions at AS. They give you a choice of four straightforward answers, of which you have to select one. For example:

1. Eighteenth-century Baroque music is usually associated with:

    ☒ **A** the electric guitar

    ☒ **B** the harpsichord

    ☒ **C** the saxophone

    ☒ **D** the synthesiser

Examiners' Tips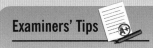

Remember there is no penalty for a wrong answer. A guess gives you a one in four chance of being right. If you don't answer you are 100% certain of not gaining a mark at all.

The correct answer is **B**. You might know it or you could work it out. Even if you don't know anything about music, you should know that synthesisers were a 20th-century invention. Guitars are ancient instruments, but electric guitars were only recently developed. Both instruments require electricity, which was unknown in the 18th century. By elimination you have reduced possible answers to two and improved your chances of answering correctly.

Multiple completion questions are rather more difficult. You are given several pieces of information, some of which are correct and others are not. The answers are combinations of solutions from which you have to select the correct one. For example:

2. Which of these statements about Galileo are correct?

   (i)   As an astrologer he used to predict the future
   (ii)   He was a talented mathematician
   (iii)   He was the first scientist to claim the universe was heliocentric
   (iv)   He invented the telescope and used it to view distant objects

   ☒ **A**   (i) and (ii)

   ☒ **B**   (i) and (iii)

   ☒ **C**   (ii) and (iii)

   ☒ **D**   (ii) and (iv)

Each of these answers might seem plausible when read quickly and you may be uncertain which is correct. You need to eliminate answers to improve your chances. Read statement (i) again carefully. Note that it refers to an astrologer. Your knowledge should tell you that Galileo was an astronomer. Therefore it is reasonable to assume that statement (i) is inaccurate and should be discarded, thus removing answers **A** and **B**. You now have to decide between **C** and **D**. Statement (ii), which is one you might have been uncertain about, is in both answers and so must be correct. By elimination you only have to choose between statements (iii) and (iv). You should have learnt that Copernicus was famous for developing the heliocentric theory. Therefore the correct answer is **D**. Even if you didn't know about Copernicus, elimination has improved your chances. It is better to guess between two possible answers rather than between three or four.

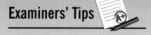

Examiners' Tips

The best way to avoid silly mistakes is to read the questions carefully and check what you are asked to do.

Tips: In the exam
- Plan your time carefully; know how much time to give to each question.
- When reading the question, cover the answers and try to anticipate the correct one.
- Read the question several times *slowly* before selecting an answer. Make sure you know exactly what you are being asked to do. If necessary rewrite the question in your own words.
- Read all possible answers before marking your choice on the answer grid.
- Don't leap at the first answer that looks right, but eliminate as many answers as possible before selecting a response.
- Remember that 'funny' responses are usually wrong.
- Be prepared to skip questions and come back to them later.
- Make sure you enter your answer clearly and only give one answer.
- Relate each alternative answer back to the stem and see if it makes sense.

Tips: At the end of the exam
- Check your answers. Only change them if you are absolutely certain.
- Don't leave any questions blank when you hand your paper in.
- If you have tried everything else, be prepared to guess.

In the AS exam you will quite often be given some data (a table of figures, a picture, graph or diagram, three or four paragraphs from a book or newspaper) and a series of questions will follow.

- In Section A (multiple choice questions) you may be asked to undertake simple number calculations or respond to specific questions about a passage of writing, mainly to test how well you understand what is being argued.
- In Section B, the data will usually be a passage of writing and the questions will probably fit into two categories: some will test comprehension/understanding while others will test thinking and analytical skills – types of knowledge and argument.
- In Section C a short piece of data will come before a question which is in reality a mini-essay in which you will need to draw on the data and interpret it – but you will almost certainly need to go beyond it to discuss a different perspective or interpretation before you reach a conclusion.

Pages 110–113 below discuss the skills you need to tackle questions on numerical data; pages 114–115 discuss the skills you need to answer Section B questions on a passage of writing.

Essential numeracy skills

In any of the AS or A2 units, questions may be set which require candidates to demonstrate application of number skills, such as:

- *undertaking number tasks* such as: addition and subtraction; multiplication and division; use of decimals and calculation of percentages; calculation of means, medians and modes; and estimation
- using *mathematical reasoning* to build up an argument
- *comprehending and interpreting data* in different forms, e.g. tables or figures, or working on a table or diagram and demonstrating that you can understand the trends it is describing and other significant details.

Number tasks

In Unit 1 you might be given information about the numbers of crimes reported and detected or, perhaps, the numbers of offenders who reoffend. Alternatively in Unit 2 you could be given data concerning election statistics, the age breakdown of supporters for particular parties and so on.

Data produced by the Office of National Statistics in *Social Trends* and similar publications, or by the Economic and Social Research Council, will typically use all of the forms of calculation listed above to create data. This data may be represented in the form of tables of figures; bar charts or histograms; line graphs; pie charts; or scatter diagrams.

You need to go into your General Studies exam with a calculator (subject to the rules of the exam). A ruler can be very useful because it makes it easier to interpret graphs or diagrams more accurately. You need to practise looking at a diagram or table and identifying exactly what it is telling you.

Many candidates in General Studies exams lose marks by not correctly stating the units in which their answer is expressed; others lose out because they put

 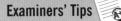

the decimal point in the wrong place or ignore a direct instruction given about the number of significant figures to which an answer is to be taken.

When you first look at data and before you start to calculate the exact answer to any question, it is a good idea to estimate in your own mind roughly what you might expect the answer to be (you need to practise doing this as part of your revision for the exam). For example, if this 'first look' suggests the answer might be about £55 million, you will know immediately if your detailed calculation comes out at £4.5 million or £600 million that something is wrong somewhere and you need to do some systematic checking.

Mathematical reasoning

This means you are not necessarily required to undertake a particular calculation, but instead you use mathematical information and reasoning to build up an argument. This may well involve ideas such as:

- simple **probability** involving combinations of independent events
- statistical measures and diagrams
- sampling and basic statistics.

Statistical measures which are particularly useful for AS General Studies students include identifying and studying a population (e.g. of people in a town or of visitors to a local holiday resort). If the process is observed at various times, this is called a *time series*; quite often we compare wages or prices monthly or annually using indices such as the *retail prices index*.

Rather than compile data about an entire population, we usually study a subset of the population, called a *sample*; we use numerical terms such as *normal* (and *non-normal*) *distributions*, *mean* and *standard deviation* to describe and apply our findings. No sample will exactly replicate characteristics of its population but, allowing for randomness, we can draw inferences about the larger population. This helps us to:

- test an hypothesis
- estimate numerical characteristics of the full population
- recognise associations between variables in the form of correlations
- develop a model of relationships.

The concept of correlation is important. Looking at data may reveal that two variables seem to vary together, for example, a study of wealth and age of death among people might suggest that poorer people tend to have shorter lives than richer people. But we cannot immediately claim the existence of a *'cause and effect' relationship* between these two variables because the cause could lie with a third, previously unconsidered, phenomenon – perhaps some form of environmental pollution or a link with smoking.

To take another example, it might be noted that people tend to wear very few clothes near orange trees during the orange-picking season and someone might try to make a link between the two. This is, in fact a *spurious correlation* because the amount of clothing we wear and the growing of oranges are both influenced by a quite different variable, i.e. the hot temperatures in the area during summer time.

Examiners' Tips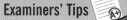

A good way to build up your skill in interpreting graphical data is to look at a recent edition of *Social Trends* (published annually). This may be downloaded free of charge from the www.statistics.gov.uk/ website, where you will find a comprehensive commentary explains or 'unpacks' the information within the various figures and tables.

Key terms

probability – the likelihood or chance that something is the case or will happen

Taking it further

To get a better idea of how a prices index works, make an index of the items that AS General studies students typically buy, and add data to it month on month.

Comprehending and interpreting data

The first and most important consideration always to bear in mind when you examine a diagram is to look at the variables being measured and the units used. Sometimes changes are portrayed so they seem to be much greater than they were in reality.

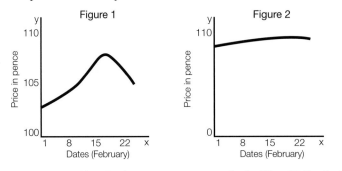

Price of petrol (per litre) at a country garage in the West Midlands, February 2008

Note that the information on the two graphs is identical, showing that the price of petrol moved from 102.5p on 1 February, to 104p on 8 February to 107.5p on 15 February to 105p on 22 February. Figure 1 seems to show a much more substantial price change, but that is because the units on the y scale go from 100p to 110p while those on Figure 2 go from 0p to 110p. Newspapers often focus attention on recent price changes by using the Figure 1 approach.

In Figures 1 and 2 there is no fixed relationship between the variables measured on the x axis and y axis. Sometimes, however, there is a relationship between the figures, and you need to understand how to interpret this. In Figure 3 you can see that a *scatter diagram* has been produced for the workforce in a factory showing the number of working days lost, cross referenced against the average number of hours worked by each worker per week; the information seems to suggest that those who work the longest hours in some cases have the poorest sickness record. Once we can see all the points on the diagram, we then produce a *line of best fit* which aims to summarise the data from all the individual cases shown to help us make an estimate or prediction of the relationship between hours worked and days lost. In this case a linear (straight line) graph is produced, implying a fixed ratio (10:20, 20:40, 30:60 or whatever) between the two variables, but in some instances a line of best fit may be curved.

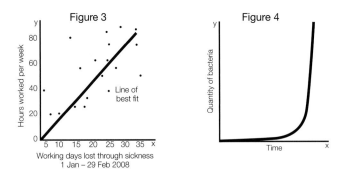

The relationship is very different in Figure 4, which shows an exponential growth curve. Here, for any exponentially growing quantity (e.g. bacteria), the larger it gets the faster it grows over time. In the case of exponential decay (e.g. decay of radioactive materials), the quantity decreases at a rate proportional to its value.

Once you are confident you can understand what a diagram or table is telling you, try to work out whether there are any *trends* to note and what possible *explanations* might account for them. Don't assume that if you have a linear (straight line) curve, it will simply carry on like that for ever. Often a question will ask you to explain the data and then either suggest *reasons* for any trends or *predict* how and why the data may change in the next 10 or 20 years.

UK population change – annual averages						
	Thousands					
	Population at start of period	Live births	Deaths	Net natural change	Net migration & other	Overall change
1951–1961	50,287	839	593	246	6	252
1961–1971	52,807	962	638	324	–12	312
1971–1981	55,928	736	666	69	–27	43
1981–1991	56,357	757	655	103	5	108
1991–2001	57,439	731	631	100	68	167
2001–2005	59,113	692	600	92	182	274
2005–2011	**60,209**	**702**	**581**	**121**	**160**	**281**
2011–2021	**61,892**	**716**	**578**	**139**	**145**	**284**

Source: Office for National Statistics; Government Actuary's Department; General Register Office for Scotland; Northern Ireland Statistics and Research Agency

Social Trends 37, Table 1.6, Office for National Statistics, 2007

Sometimes (as in the table above) government statistics include predictions or **extrapolations** for later years. But the results are speculative and can only be as strong as the assumptions on which they are based. The population data in the table is particularly useful because in this case we can see how the predicted numbers for 2005–2011 and 2011–2021 are arrived at. The overall changes for these periods are really no more than 'best guesses':

Key terms

extrapolation – the process of constructing new data points outside a set of known data points

- Although we have information about the *birth rate* in recent years, we cannot be sure whether there will be a modest increase. Perhaps the birth rate among people newly arrived in the UK will prove higher than that for people who have always lived here.
- We have plenty of information about *mortality rates* and *life expectancy*, but a new bout of hospital infections or a world-wide killer flu pandemic or – to be more optimistic – the discovery of a new, life-extending wonder drug could make us change the assumptions previously made.
- Similarly the assumptions about *immigration* and *emigration* policy may turn out to be false. People who have come to the UK from Eastern Europe may decide to return to their home countries rather than stay once they have built up a nest-egg for their future.

So the best way to evaluate predictions such as those in the table is to find out all about the assumptions on which the predictions are based, subject them to rigorous testing and scrutiny and then monitor carefully how closely 'real life' matches the predictions made.

How to read and analyse Section B passages

Data response questions are usually based on a passage such as the one below.

Where's the politics?

An Inconvenient Truth, the Oscar-winning film about global warming produced by former US Vice President Al Gore, was acclaimed so much that the government wanted to provide free copies to schools for use in subjects such as General Studies and PSHE. Then, Mr Dimmock, a school governor from Kent, found out about the film and went to court in October 2007 to try and prevent it from being shown in UK schools, claiming it was biased.

The judge identified various claimed inaccuracies in the film and said that if it is shown, the government must first amend their *Guidance Notes to Teachers* to make it clear that the film is a political work promoting only one side of the argument and that teachers who present the film without making this plain could be guilty of political indoctrination.

Although Mr Dimmock claimed he simply wanted the best for his children, Jamie Doward (Home Affairs Editor of *The Observer*, writing on 14 October 2007) pointed out that Mr Dimmock was funded by a Scottish quarrying magnate who established a controversial lobbying group to attack environmentalists' claims about global warming. So it is possible the rich employer paid for the court case because the message from the film conflicted with his business interests. Maybe Mr Dimmock's claims were just as political as he claimed the film to be.

There are some key questions a reader always needs to consider when reading a passage or article; they are certainly very relevant to this passage:

- Is it based on *fact* or *opinion*?
- Is the *evidence* in the article strong enough to be believable?
- Does the article give *both sides of an argument* or just one?
- When it reaches a *conclusion* how well is it justified?
- Are *reasons* for the conclusion clearly given and are they explicitly *explained*?
- In what ways might the article be regarded as *controversial*?
- Could the article have been written by someone who is promoting a political or business *interest* to try and influence the reader to the writer's advantage?

Many of these questions or considerations were raised earlier in this book (see pages 5–8).

Assessment objectives

The questions on any passage given to you in the exam are designed to test your competence in any or all of the four assessment objectives. The exact balance of marks, in terms of assessment objectives, in Section B in any one Unit 1 or Unit 2 paper may vary slightly, but a typical arrangement would be:

AO1	*Demonstrate* relevant knowledge and understanding applied to a range of issues, *using* skills from different disciplines	9 marks
AO2	*Marshal* evidence and draw conclusions: *select, interpret, evaluate and integrate* information, data, concepts and opinions	9 marks
AO3	*Demonstrate* understanding of different types of knowledge, *appreciating* their strengths and limitations	7 marks
AO4	*Communicate clearly* and accurately in a concise, logical and relevant way	5 marks

AO1

Sometimes a passage may contain quite detailed descriptions or details, in which case the extent to which you demonstrate you have understood these, and any implications, in the answers you write will be marked by AO1. You particularly need to keep in mind the relevance of the points made by the writer to support the conclusions s/he reaches. If some of the points made simply do not fit into the rest of the discussion, that would be a weakness.

AO2

AO2 marks are awarded for your analysis of the passage. How well has the writer organised the material? How clearly can you recognise the writer's plan for the piece? Sometimes writers follow this approach: 'Say what you are going to say, say it and say what you have said.' As a result, the article or extract has some coherence, making it easier for the reader to understand. Is the issue addressed in a sufficiently comprehensive manner? Are ideas consistent and well backed up by evidence? Referring to concepts such as freedom, democracy, fairness and honesty can be particularly impressive, especially if ideas and evidence are appropriately linked together. Of course, even if a strong claim is made, possibly well backed up by good evidence, you may be unconvinced by the way the writer develops, interprets or evaluates this; if this is the case, you need to explain why in simple, clear terms.

AO3

If the whole passage seems one-sided or to contain too many opinions (particularly if they do not come from known authorities), or to be based on insufficient factual content, you should say so if you are asked to comment on the information or the arguments; this will gain you AO3 marks. Once you have analysed the different types of argument (inductive, deductive, etc.) used by the writer, remember that deductive arguments are regarded as being more reliably true than inductive arguments, so you should have greater confidence in a conclusion which is supported by deductive arguments.

AO4

AO4 marks are awarded for your communication skills in analysing and commenting on the passage; they come from the accuracy of language and appropriateness of structure in your answers. Writing neatly in black (or blue) ink, organising your answers into sentences and paragraphs, and writing good English will help you achieve good marks.

To sum up, when you see there is a passage on which questions are based:

- Note the title and consider how relevant it is to the whole of the piece (it may cover only part of the piece).
- Identify the main argument and how the writer justifies it (note the evidence, argument, etc.).
- If there seems to be a considerable amount of assertion (claims without evidence or other support), be sceptical and say so if you get a chance to do so relevantly.
- Consider whether there is a counter argument, and whether it is presented to give the piece of writing a genuine balance.
- Ask whether the writer gives you a good enough reason to understand why one argument is preferred to the other.
- Identify the writer's conclusion and consider whether it links closely enough to the arguments and evidence presented.

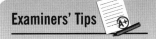

Examiners' Tips

Use the glossary in this book, as well as your experience in studying other AS level subjects, to become familiar with the concepts that writers might want to refer to.

Examiners' Tips

When you use the passage to help you answer the questions, always use your own words, not the writer's.

Sample questions and answers 1

This passage and the questions which follow could appear on a Unit 1 paper.

WILL THEY BE CRIMINALS IN LATER LIFE?

The director of forensic sciences at Scotland Yard, Gary Pugh, has said that primary school children should be listed on the DNA database if they show behaviour which suggests they might become criminals when they are older. He said some experts believe it is possible to detect behaviour in children as young as five that might suggest they would offend in the future.

'If we have a primary means of identifying people before they offend, then in the long-term the benefits of targeting younger people are extremely large,' Pugh told the Observer newspaper. 'You could argue the younger the better. Criminologists say some people will grow out of crime; others won't. We have to find who are possibly going to be the biggest threat to society.' Pugh also acknowledged that the contentious idea raises serious issues about the role of teachers in recognising children who might be future offenders, about objections from parents to the measures and about possible labelling in the future, but said society needed to honestly discuss how best to prevent crime.

A report from the Institute for Public Policy Research, entitled 'Make me a Criminal', takes a more therapeutic approach to preventing youth offending. The report makes a case for providing support for children between the ages of 5 and 12, including cognitive behavioural therapy, parenting programmes and intensive educational interventions. The report suggested that prevention should start young, because prolific offenders typically start early – between the ages of 10 and 13. The author of the report, Julia Margo, told the Observer, 'You can carry out a risk factor analysis where you look at the characteristics of an individual child aged 5 to 7 and identify risk factors that make it more likely that they would become an offender.' However, she also told the Observer that listing such children on a database risked stigmatising them by identifying them in a negative way.

Shami Chakrabarti, director of the civil rights group Liberty, condemned the suggestion to target youngsters. She told the Observer, 'The British public is highly respectful of the police…but playing politics with our innocent kids is a step too far.' Her view was shared by Chris Davis of the National Headteachers' Association, who felt teachers and parents might find the idea potentially dangerous. He added, 'It is condemning them [children] at a very young age to something they have not yet done. They may have the potential to do something, but we all have the potential to do things.' Davis also said that most teachers could recognise when children 'had the potential to have a more challenging adult life,' but said a teacher's role is to support them.

So on balance, while a preventative approach to crime is good, the practical damage that might be caused by suggesting children will be criminal in later life is potentially too great.

(a) Using your own knowledge, briefly explain the **benefits** of placing a sample of a child's DNA on the police database.

(2 marks)

(b) Using the passage, who would be likely to **oppose** a proposal to place the DNA of all primary school children on the police database?

(2 marks)

(c) Using the passage and your own knowledge:

(i) what objections could be advanced to oppose putting children's DNA on a police database?

(4 marks)

(ii) how far and on what grounds could support be given to objections to putting children's DNA on a police database?

(4 marks)

Quality of written communication (3)

QUESTION (a)

Alice's answer	Matthew's answer
The more people on the DNA database, the more chance that wrongdoers will be detected.	There is a very high proportion of crimes for which the offender is never identified or punished. Although there are concerns about putting DNA from young children on the database, it would help track down offenders. If everyone's DNA was on record, the chances of apprehending many more criminals would be greatly increased.

Examiner assessment: Alice would probably gain 1 mark, though her answer is very short and she has not included much knowledge of her own. Matthew would be awarded 2 marks for a fuller answer, including good points about detection rates.

QUESTION (b)

Alice's answer	Matthew's answer
The parents and the children themselves.	The passage says parents would be likely to object, so would civil rights groups such as Liberty led by Shami Chakrabarti and, if headteacher Chris Davis is to be believed, teachers would also be critical.

Examiner assessment: Alice would probably gain 0 marks: she is right to mention parents but the children themselves are less likely to have a full enough understanding of what is involved to complain meaningfully. Matthew would be awarded 2 marks for a fuller answer, which shows he has achieved a good understanding of the passage.

QUESTION (c)

Alice's answer	Matthew's answer
(i) Children cannot be found responsible for a criminal offence until they are aged at least 10 so it seems wrong to put the names of younger children on the database. Placing children on a database risks stigmatising them by identifying them in a negative way. Also, putting names on a database is condemning children at a very young age to something they have not yet done.	(i) In a way putting a child's name on the DNA database would be like punishing them in case they do wrong at some stage rather than because they have already done so. If some children's names were placed on the database and others were not, those who were listed might be regarded as trouble-makers and this might even become part of their self-image or identity, a self-fulfilling prophecy for future poor behaviour, perhaps.
(ii) Many people believe that all adults and children over an age (e.g. 10 years) should be on the database to catch criminals. If this happened there wouldn't be a need to object because everyone would be in the same position.	(ii) The points made in the passage by Julia Margo highlight fears of stigmatising particular groups of very young children who are below the age of criminal liability. Such opposition is very worthy of support. The principal case against putting names on the DNA database is mainly about civil rights. There is also the practical difficulty of selecting young children to be put on the database if teachers refuse to see such a selection as part of their professional responsibility.

Examiner assessment: (i) Alice would probably gain 2 marks: her first point is excellent, but her other two points are weakened by the fact that she is not using her own words. Matthew would be awarded 3 marks for a simple but fuller answer which is expressed in his own words. (ii) Alice produces a simple and logical but not very complete answer and would be awarded 2 marks. Matthew's answer is much fuller, making excellent points about stigmatising the young, civil rights and the role of teachers: he would score 4 marks. Communication: Alice would probably get 2 marks and Matthew 3.

Overall: Alice would have 7/15 and Matthew 14/15

Sample questions and answers 2

This passage and the questions which follow could appear on a Unit 2 paper.

Will readers and viewers ever want to trust the media again?

Controversial remarks by Channel 4's Jon Snow attacking the media embargo of Prince Harry's service in Afghanistan attracted a fierce backlash. Snow was against the news blackout which was tantamount to censorship, believing that journalists should have reported Prince Harry's deployment to Afghanistan – even if it put lives at risk.

In a mass email, Snow commended the Drudge Report, a website in the USA, which broke the news and forced the Ministry of Defence to confirm it. 'Editors have been sworn to secrecy over Prince Harry being sent to fight in Afghanistan three months ago…[and] Drudge has blown their cover,' he wrote. He continued to question the news blackout – despite the fact that Channel 4 had agreed to abide by it. An unrepentant Snow robustly defended himself in an interview with Radio 4's Today programme. He said: 'I think the decision to keep information from the viewer and listener is a very serious one and it goes to the very root of the issue of trust between the media and the consumers.'

His comments triggered a furious response from former royal aides and also military figures. Dickie Arbiter, a former very popular press secretary to the Queen, commented: 'There was a famous slogan: "Careless Talk Costs Lives". It seems like someone probably resurrected that with Harry going to Afghanistan and came to a very apt arrangement.' Colonel Jorge Mendonca, who served in Iraq, said: 'What planet is he living on? As the BBC has pointed out, they have similar arrangements when the Prime Minister visits a war zone. That's to enable him to do his job safely, just as this deal has done.' So why would the approach that works for Gordon Brown not be just as right for Prince Harry?

Retired Major General Patrick Cordingley, who led the Desert Rats into Iraq during the first Gulf War, said: 'I have a deep respect for Jon Snow, but I did feel that this time he was off the mark. I applauded the media…It certainly wasn't censorship – it was purely voluntarily.'

The blackout was put in place and Prince Harry came home safely as a result. Yet censorship is censorship whether imposed upon us by others or by ourselves – and censorship surely isn't compatible with a free society, no matter how good the reasons for it may be.

(a)   Using your own knowledge, define and give an example of 'censorship'.

(1 mark)

(b)   Using the third paragraph, write out **two** facts.

(1 mark)

(c)   Using the fourth and fifth paragraphs, write out **two** opinions.

(2 marks)

(d)   (i)   What is an argument from analogy?

(1 mark)

       (ii)   Write out an example of an argument from analogy from the passage.

(1 mark)

(e)   State and give an example of one other type of argument used in the passage.

(2 marks)

(f)   How far and in what ways do the evidence and arguments introduced by the writer support the statement at the end of the passage: 'censorship surely isn't compatible with a free society, no matter how good the reasons for it may be'?

(4 marks)

You are not being asked to give your own opinions but to use thinking and analytical skills to examine the passage.

Quality of written communication (3)

QUESTION (a)

Sumita's answer
When the media are prevented from publishing particular items, this is known as censorship. A form of censorship occurs when the censor classifies films but the most important kind is to protect Official Secrets, for example by issuing a D Notice, to protect national security.

Kenny's answer
Censorship is when the government issues a D Notice.

Examiner assessment: Sumita gives both definition and examples (in fact just one example was required) so she will be awarded 1 mark. Kenny gives an example but not a definition, so he gets 0 marks.

QUESTION (b)

Sumita's answer
(i)   Dickie Arbiter, (is) a former very popular press secretary to the Queen
(ii)   Harry going (went) to Afghanistan

Kenny's answer
(i)   Snow commended the Drudge website in the USA
(ii)   Editors had been sworn to secrecy

Examiner assessment: Sumita's first example becomes an opinion (not a fact) when she includes the words 'very popular'; her second example is correct but she needs to have identified two facts to gain a mark so her score is 0. Kenny gains no marks because he has taken both his perfectly correct examples from the second rather than the third paragraph.

QUESTION (c)

Sumita's answer

(i) I have a deep respect for Jon Snow

(ii) this time he was off the mark

Kenny's answer

(i) it certainly wasn't censorship – it was purely voluntarily

(ii) censorship surely isn't compatible with a free society

Examiner assessment: Sumita and Kenny both gain 2 marks for correctly identifying two opinions.

QUESTION (d)

Sumita's answer

(i) It is a kind of reasoning based on apparent similarities between two things. It is saying that because of the supposed similarity in one aspect they will probably be similar in other aspects.

(ii) 'They have similar arrangements when the Prime Minister visits a war zone. That's to enable him to do his job safely, just as this deal one done.' So why would the approach that works for Gordon Brown not be just as right for Prince Harry?

Kenny's answer

(i) It is a form of parallel reasoning where one thing is the same as another.

(ii) Colonel Jorge Mendonca, who served in Iraq, said: 'What planet is he living on? As the BBC has pointed out, they have similar arrangements when the Prime Minister visits a war zone. That's to enable him to do his job safely, just as this deal has done.' So why would the approach that works for Gordon Brown not be just as right for Prince Harry?

Examiner assessment: Sumita gains 2 marks but Kenny gets none. Kenny makes the mistake of not spelling out his first answer with sufficient clarity, and in the second he writes out a longer extract from the third paragraph than he should have, suggesting he didn't realise the first three lines of his answer were not an analogy and so not required.

QUESTION (e)

Sumita's answer

Causal argument – 'The blackout was put in place … Prince Harry came home safely as a result.'

Kenny's answer

Inductive argument – the writer makes some observations and then comes to a conclusion.

Examiner assessment: Sumita gains 2 marks but Kenny gains only 1 mark. Causal argument (Sumita's answer) is acceptable here but it is a very weak form of argument in this context. Inductive argument is better but Kenny needed to have been a bit more explicit about the conclusion reached as a result of the observations. Kenny would have gained 2 marks if he had included a clear example.

QUESTION (f)

Sumita's answer

Discussions about censorship are always something of a balancing act. The idea of restricting free speech is unwelcome in a democratic country such as Britain but sometimes there are stronger circumstances which justify it, for example if we are concerned with the personal safety of the Prime Minister or Prince Harry.

The quote says 'censorship surely isn't compatible with a free society, no matter how good the reasons for it may be' but the key lies in the final ten words – sometimes the reasons <u>are</u> good enough to justify a news blackout. If a country such as Britain never censored anything, there could be times when we allowed sensitive diplomatic or commercial information to reach people who would not have our country's best interests at heart.

To that extent, if the reasons are good enough (but not if they are frivolous or if it is done to avoid someone mild embarrassment), I believe that even a free society is justified in censoring the spread of some information.

Kenny's answer

Few people are keen on censorship but even so if it protects the lives of soldiers (not just Prince Harry but the ordinary squaddies he served with in Afghanistan) then it is justified. Better to have censorship and live than not have it and maybe die.

Also sometimes a free society needs to use censorship to protect its official secrets and matters of national security from the intelligence operatives from other countries – James Bond might not be about to save the world that day.

Examiner assessment: Sumita has produced a good, well-written answer and will receive 4 marks (+3 for communication skills). Kenny's answer is much shorter and a bit colloquial so he will gain 2 marks (+2 for communication skills).

Overall Sumita has scored 14/15 and Kenny 8/15

Practice questions: Unit 1

This passage and the questions which follow could appear on a Unit 1 paper. A mark scheme for this question can be found on page 157.

Concern in Europe on Cellphone Ads for Children

The MO1 beginner mobile phone is not as cuddly as a teddy bear, but manufacturers of the curvy crimson-and-blue handset for 6-year-olds promise a similarly warm and fuzzy relationship...Yet such shiny child-size phones are stirring some parental and

5 government unease...The year 2006 was the turning point when the telephone industry started focusing not just on teenagers and adults but also on 'tweens' – children between middle childhood and adolescence, about 8 to 12 years old – and even children as young as 5. Bright new 'kiddie' telephones began appearing on the

10 market that can speed-dial grandma and grandpa with a click of a button.

The MO1...prompted some parent groups in Europe to demand a government ban on marketing to children...The objections are driven in part by a lack of knowledge about the long-term health

15 effects of mobile phone use...An environmental advocacy group for young people in Spain, argues that 'the mobile telephone industry is acting like the tobacco industry by designing products that addict the very young'...In France the health minister, Roselyne Bachelot, has taken such concerns public...urging

20 parents to limit use, reducing children's telephone calls to no more than six minutes... 'I believe in the principle of precaution,' Ms. Bachelot said in an interview. 'If there is a risk, then children with developing nervous systems would be affected. I've alerted parents about the use of mobile telephones because it's absurd for young

25 children to have them.'

For most parents, decisions about cellphones are driven by other concerns. When his daughter Morgan was 12 years old, Greg Pozgar...resisted buying a mobile phone for her, mostly because he was worried she might run up a huge bill...Morgan received her

30 first phone as a Christmas gift and went on to become a champion of text messaging at age 13 in a national $25,000 competition organized last year by telephone manufacturer LG...Mr. Pozgar – who had been coaching football for 17 years – has noticed that lately more of his 8- and 9-year old players are packing mobile

35 telephones. 'I don't necessarily think that's a bad thing,' he said. 'But how does a kid that old seem responsible enough...My gosh, then can barely remember to tie their shoes.'

Doreen Carvajal, from the New York Times, *8th March 2008* © *2008*

(a) Using your own knowledge, briefly explain **two** reasons why phones for 'tweens' (line 7) might be regarded as a good idea.

(3 marks)

(b) Using the paragraphs 2 and 3 of the passage, state and briefly explain **two** reasons why phones for 'tweens' (line 7) might be regarded as a bad idea.

(3 marks)

(c) Briefly explain why some parent groups might consider a marketing ban (line 13) was desirable.

(3 marks)

(d) From the second paragraph, briefly explain why a government minister should get involved in a debate about mobile phones for children.

(3 marks)

(e) (i) What type of argument is used in lines 15–18 of the second paragraph?

(1 mark)

(ii) How persuasive is this form of argument **both** in this case **and** generally?

(3 marks)

Quality of written communication (3 marks)

Practice questions: Unit 2

This passage and the questions which follow could appear on a Unit 2 paper. A mark scheme for this question can be found on page 158.

Are we teachers or parents?

The end of the traditional family means that schools are increasingly taking the place of parents in providing guidance to children, Dr John Dunford warned yesterday. Dr Dunford, a former headteacher and the general secretary of the Association
5 of School and College Leaders (ASCL), was speaking yesterday at ASCL's annual conference in Brighton. 'For some children, schools have had to take the place of the institutions that used to set the boundaries of acceptable behaviour – that was, fundamentally, the family and the church', Dunford said. 'Never
10 have the values of school been more important in children's lives. Never has the job of school leaders in articulating those values… been so important.'

Dunford suggested that many children now lack basic social skills, such as holding simple conversations or using a knife and
15 fork. Others suffered serious behavioural problems because of the lack of a stable home life. For many children, school is 'the only solid bedrock in their lives' where they are given clear moral boundaries.

According to official figures from the Office for National
20 Statistics, there were 1.84 million lone parents in Britain in 2007 compared with 1.59 million in 1997. 1.69 million were single mothers (up from 1.45 million a decade earlier), many of whom are being pressured by government to get a job to help combat labour shortages and to earn money rather than live off benefits,
25 so that means the number of single men raising children has increased from 140,000 to 150,000. The figures suggest that marriage breakdown has increased in southern England but not in the north.

'Schools can't and shouldn't replace the role of parents', Dunford
30 said, adding: 'It's perhaps a sad indictment on the present age that we accept the need to help parents to play their part – to rediscover what being a parent means.'

His comments come after demands by ministers that schools should target parents who – for whatever reason – do not show
35 sufficient interest in their children's education.

Yet the question remains – if the family no longer works as it did, who better than teachers to fill the gap and make sure children are equipped to function as balanced adults in our modern society?

(a)   Write out **one** fact from the first sentence.

(1 mark)

(b)   Why might the extract be seen as an argument from authority?

(1 mark)

(c)   Why might the writers talk of 'the end of the traditional family' (line 1) and claim that 'the family no longer works as it did' (line 36)?

(2 marks)

(d)   Give **two** examples of what is meant by 'clear moral boundaries' (line 17).

(2 marks)

(e)   (i)   What type of argument is used in the third paragraph (lines 20–26) where the writers state:

'… there were 1.84 million lone parents in Britain in 2007 compared with 1.59 million in 1997. 1.69 million were single mothers (up from 1.45 million a decade earlier) … so that means the number of single men raising children has risen from 140,000 to 150,000'?

(1 mark)

(ii)   Consider whether inductive arguments or deductive arguments are the more effective form of argument in supporting a conclusion.

(2 marks)

(f)   How far would it be a fair criticism of the passage to say it contains too many opinions and not enough facts for a case to be established effectively?

(4 marks)

You are not being asked to give your own opinions but to use thinking and analytical skills to examine the passage.

Quality of written communication (3 marks)

Activity

Plan a time line for answering either Unit 1 or Unit 2. Show clearly the time you would spend on each section and on each extended writing question.

Examiners' Tips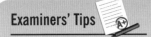

One of the things an examiner will look for is the additional value that you bring either to the stimulus material or to the essay structure.

Examiners' Tips

Note carefully whether you are being asked to use your own knowledge or to examine evidence contained in a passage, table or other stimulus material.

Almost 60% (54 out of 90 marks) of the assessment is based on extended writing. All of Section C and approximately half of Section B test this important skill. About 14 of these marks will be used to assess your communication skills (AO4). As an indication of the amount of writing you are expected to produce, each of the extended writing questions in Section B is allocated about one side of the answer book, and the two questions in Section C are allocated two sides each. Obviously you do not have to fill this space unless you want to and you can work on extra paper if you find it necessary. You should expect to spend no more than 10 minutes on the Section B questions and about 20 minutes on each of the Section C questions.

It is in the extended writing pieces, especially in Section C, that you have some freedom to shape your answer as you wish, although obviously it must be within the structure and topic set by the examiner. This freedom will enable you to select the evidence you use to support your answer; it will also give you a wonderful opportunity to demonstrate the quality of your own thinking and the way you are able to select and apply information. Make sure that you take advantage of the opportunities that exist, because it is largely on the way you handle these questions that your final grade will depend.

Types of extended writing

You must use the correct type of writing to meet the demands of the question you are answering. You are given clues as to the approach you should use in each question. When faced with any question requiring extended writing you should ask yourself, 'What is the examiner's purpose in asking this question?' Another important question is what evidence you should use in your answer. You will not gain marks if you ignore instructions and fail to do what has been asked of you.

The main types of extended writing used in General Studies are:

Descriptive *(e.g. 'How did Copernicus change the way in which scientists understand our place in the universe?')*
This type of question is designed to allow you to show what you know and understand about a particular issue. Key command words used to introduce this type of question may include 'describe', 'give an account of', 'use your own knowledge to show', 'in what ways', 'how does' or 'give details of'. To answer this type of question effectively you must be able to demonstrate clear knowledge of the topic or issue. Make sure that you do not simply pour out everything you know and that everything you include is relevant to the question.

Opinion *(e.g. '"The purpose of science is to discover new knowledge and improve the quality of life." Which of these do you consider to be the more important? Explain your answer.')*
Sometimes you will be presented with a topic and asked to give your own ideas and thoughts about it. If you are answering this type of question, remember to use evidence to support your ideas. It is easy to give opinions on almost any subject, but they will only convince a reader if they are supported and

justified. If you are asked, 'Should river fishing be banned?' it is very easy to answer 'Yes I think it should.' But very few anglers would be convinced by this. However, if you say, 'Yes I think it should, because ...' and then give your reasons with supporting evidence, you will at least give your reader something to think about. Your audience may not agree with what you say, but will have to consider your ideas. Command words used for this type of question could include 'how far do you agree', 'to what extent ' or 'justify the view that'.

Analytical (e.g. 'Assess claims that owners of the mass media have too much influence.')

These questions are usually based on data which you are required to examine critically. Command words may include 'analyse', 'examine', 'consider', 'how does the author', 'what are the strengths and weaknesses of', 'does the author provide enough evidence', ' identify evidence which' or 'assess'. You will not gain many marks simply by selecting information or copying content from the passage (if there is one) or putting it into your own words, or even by simply presenting information about the topic. Certainly you should present or identify the required information, but you must consider it critically and ask how far it actually does what it is intended to do in the context you have been given. At the simplest level, you should be able to consider the relative strengths or weaknesses of the evidence and its sufficiency.

Explanation (e.g. 'Explain why education is regarded as an important form of socialisation.')

This type of question will provide you with information or refer you to a key issue and ask you to explain it and say why it is significant or why it occurred. Command words used might include 'explain', 'give reasons for', 'why', 'suggest why' or 'account for'. The number of marks should give you an idea of how many different points you will be expected to make. In an 'explain' answer you are not expected to provide a great deal of description, but you should use sufficient evidence to show that you do have a sound understanding of the issue. Unless you are asked to do so, do not reject or argue against the issue that is the focus of the question.

Argument (e.g. 'Critically examine arguments for and against the view that despite recent legislation there is no such thing as equality of opportunity.')

In this type of question you are given a provocative idea or statement. Your task is to present a 'debate' on the subject, i.e. present and critically examine opposing viewpoints using supporting evidence to reach and justify a conclusion. You must weigh up the evidence (evaluate it) to see which perspective receives the most convincing support. In answering this type of question you need to recognise that different perspectives are justifiable and to adopt a balanced and unbiased view. An important part of the answer is the conclusion you reach. You must be careful not to adopt an emotional or one-sided approach. Avoid making assertions which you cannot support with evidence. Command words used in these questions include 'assess arguments for and against', 'how far can the view x be justified (or supported)', 'consider the view that', 'critically examine these conflicting views' and 'examine claims that'. If you are presenting an argument it is natural that you will have your own opinions, but do not let these get in the way of a fair and balanced consideration of different viewpoints.

Activity

For each of the essays given above as examples, list evidence that would help you to answer them.

Persuasive (e.g. *'Write a letter to a local newspaper supporting the use of free range foods as evidence of a responsible society.'*)
In this type of writing you will be expected to convince a reader of a particular view. Unlike the argument it does not require the presentation of different views, but you will need to use evidence to support your claims and may use emotive language to persuade your audience. However, do not use rhetoric instead of evidence or sound argument. Command words might include 'how might you', 'support', 'persuade', 'oppose' or 'convince'.

Planning your answer

Careful planning is an important part of writing. You might think it is a waste of time to plan your answer when there is little time available. Sensible and thoughtful planning can in fact save time and will give you a better chance of answering a question correctly. It is through planning that you (a) decide what the question is asking you to do and (b) select and organise the material to use in your answer. Above all, planning enables you to produce a structured answer which will convince your reader.

A helpful way to start is to ask yourself, 'What am I being asked to do?' It sometimes helps to rewrite the question in your own words to clarify what it is about. Take note of key terms, qualifying words and command words. Each of these will help you understand what the examiner is looking for.

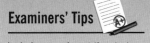

Examiners' Tips

Include your plan at the start of your answer, rather than on a separate sheet of paper. This makes it easy to refer to and means it will also be available for the examiner to see. If you cross things out, make sure they can still be read.

Candidates use different types of plans. You could use a stream of consciousness plan: when you have decided what the question is about simply list down everything that comes into your mind. Anything that is irrelevant can be crossed out and the remaining items can then be organised in the order they are to be considered. Flow or spider diagrams are clearer and better organised methods of planning. Some candidate produce tables, especially where the question asks them to examine different arguments or points of view. Whichever method you use, remember that your plan should be brief, clear and to the point.

There should always be three clear sections to any piece of extended writing:

- *Introduction* This should be brief and should set the scene for the remainder of your answer. In it you need to outline what you have been asked to do; explain the meaning of any key terms; possibly give a tentative conclusion. This section is based on your planning and will allow you to take control of the essay by explaining what you understand by the question and the parameters within which you are going to work. In order to write an effective introduction it is essential that you spend time analysing the question.
- *The main body* In this section you will present the evidence and arguments that will allow you to answer the question. The style of this section must be appropriate to the type of question you are dealing with. Any evidence you use should be accurate, specific and relevant. If you are presenting an argument, then you must ensure that you address both sides in a balanced, unbiased way, supporting the points you make with appropriate evidence and evaluating the weight of the evidence and arguments in terms of the question. If you do not know specific evidence, it can help if you describe the type of evidence needed to support your point and how you could verify it. Your material should be organised in such a way that it enables you to draw a sound conclusion.

- *Conclusion* This should arise from the main body of the answer. Do not introduce new material, but draw attention to the evidence and arguments that support your claims and point out possible weaknesses in other evidence. Try to avoid 'sitting on the fence' or reaching a conclusion that is a personal opinion rather than one that emerges from your writing.

Communicating with your reader

Remember that how you write is as important as what you write. Each piece of extended writing has communication as well as content marks, including:

- *Spelling, punctuation and grammar* You will not be expected to spell perfectly, but it is important that poor or inadequate spelling does not get in the way of meaning. Your work must be organised in paragraphs and written in complete sentences. Sentences should start with a capital letter and end with a full stop. Unless intended for a special effect, paragraphs which consist of a single sentence do not create a positive impression. Each paragraph should deal with a separate idea and reflect a specific stage of your answer.
- *Clear, coherent and concise* Aim to write clearly so that what you have to say can be easily understood and makes sense. The examiner does not want to re-read your work in order to understand your meaning. Make sure that your writing is logical and consistent. Be careful not to go off at a tangent. Make sure that you are concise. Long answers are not necessarily better than short answers and will not always achieve higher marks. Use the number of lines provided in the answer book as a guide to the amount that a person with average sized writing might be expected to produce.
- *Legibility* It doesn't matter how good your ideas are if an examiner cannot read what you have written. Very large or extremely small handwriting is very difficult to read. If the examiner has to concentrate on deciphering what you have written it is possible that your ideas and knowledge will be obscured. Use black or dark blue ink. Make sure you write on the lines provided in the answer book and don't stray into the margins.
- *Structure* There must be a clear and logical structure to what you write. Make sure that your ideas follow on from each other. Ideally readers should be able to write out a plan of what you have written and should be able to see how your thought processes and use of evidence have developed.
- *Relevance* Communication skills include relevance. Even if you have written in the most beautifully expressed English and have made no spelling, punctuation or grammatical errors, you will not score marks for communication if your material is not relevant to the question.
- *Language* Extended writing is a formal activity and requires formal language. Do not use familiar, slang or colloquial expressions or text language. In particular do not use offensive or obscene language.

If you use accepted conventions in your writing and communicate in a clear, concise and coherent manner you will gain marks. The mark descriptor for the top communication mark is *'The answer is clear and lucid (writing in the correct form is taken as a matter of course), arguments are coherent, well laid out and relevant, and there are very few grammatical or spelling errors.'*

7. almost 80% of the population still claim to be Christian in surveys and census returns
8. fills a gap in children's experience with the decline of church attendance
9. faith schools exist for parents who want specific religious teaching for their children
10. in spite of statistics we are primarily a secular society – no longer relevant
11. as a multi-faith/multi-cultural society it is unfair to many families
12. it loses value because it has to be bland and broadly based
13. many parents and teachers are opposed to both compulsion and religious education
14. it is the most resented subject by pupils and is often poorly taught
15. no other subject (apart from citizenship) is given the same level of protection
16. parents can opt children out if they wish
17. students over 16 cannot opt out for themselves: it has to be a parental decision
18. similar moral values could be taught without the religious aspects.

AO2 (marshal evidence and draw conclusions) 8 marks
Award up to 3 marks for relevant arguments within each of the following areas, up to an overall maximum of 8 marks. Reserve 2 marks for evaluative comment.

Why should RE be compulsory? E.g.:
- it is an essential part of British culture
- it can help with creating an integrated society
- it can help establish a common value system
- if it were not compulsory many schools would omit it altogether and so deprive children of entitlement

Why should RE not be compulsory? E.g.:
- it is no longer relevant in a secular age
- religion is a personal matter and should be left to families
- no other subject is compulsory after KS3; children should be able to choose
- teaching religion is an infringement of individual freedom

Should RE be 'broadly Christian'? Allow items not credited above. E.g.:
- 'broadly Christian' is a meaningless term for believers and non-believers
- many other religions in the UK also have much of value to teach
- Christian teachings (however broad) may be offensive to other religions
- it is potentially divisive.

COMMENTARY

Take note of the command words in the question. 'Examine' means more than just list or state reasons for something. You must do this, but you must also consider the points you make critically. Do they offer strong or weak reasons for the position taken? Note that you are asked to examine arguments for and against the provision of compulsory RE in state schools. It is important that your answer is balanced and gives equal consideration to both points of view. Because there are two points of view, your answer must reach a conclusion based on your assessment of the different points of view you have considered.

When analysing the question, remember to look for any key terms that need to be explained and which should influence your answer. There are really four critical terms for you to consider: (i) compulsory; (ii) broadly Christian; (iii)

Activity

Before you read the commentary, use the mark schemes to assess the quality of these answers. What are their strengths and weaknesses?

religious education; and (iv) state schools. Each of these expressions gives you a clue to the type of information that you need to include in your answer. You should also pay attention to the passage used to introduce the question. It may provide you with a context for the question as well as give you background information that may help you shape your answer. It may help you to rephrase the question to make sure that you really understand what you are being asked to do. One way of doing this is to break the question into different parts. These might be:

1. What reasons might be given to justify compulsory RE?
2. What reasons might be given to argue against compulsory RE?
3. Why 'broadly Christian'?
4. What evidence might support each point of view?
5. Which evidence provides the strongest and the weakest support?

Remember that there are three sets of marks for this question. You will be assessed on AO1 and AO2 for the content and structure of the essay and on AO4 for your communication skills. If you want to achieve high marks you must do well in all three parts. (For the Assessment Objective descriptors see page 114.)

Answer 1

This is a one-sided answer: the candidate has ignored the issue of reasons for making RE compulsory and has simply given arguments against. There is some attempt to deal with whether the subject should be 'broadly Christian' but this is not developed. The answer contains too much personal feeling, which helps to make the answer unbalanced.

There are a number of good reasons advanced which would give an AO1 mark of 4/8. (These are indicated in the text as *[1]*, *[2]* etc.)

There is limited evidence to suggest the candidate has marshalled evidence in order to draw a conclusion. The initial conclusion is based on personal prejudice rather than an evaluation of different reasons. The candidate gains marks for claiming religion is no longer relevant and should be a matter of personal choice left to families. Another mark is gained for pointing the lack of choice after GCE, giving the maximum of 3 marks for this section. Another mark is awarded for indicating that other religions exist and may be offended by Christian teachings. There is insufficient evidence of evaluation to justify further marks. For AO2 the candidate gained 4/8 marks.

Communication is reasonably clear and coherent and most of the answer is relevant. Punctuation is sound but there are careless spelling errors. The answer is both structured and paragraphed. It is awarded 2/4 AO4 marks but almost got 3.

Total marks 10/20

Answer 2

This answer has tried to look at arguments for and against and has made several good points; however the approach is much more about describing or listing reasons rather than examining them in a critical fashion. There is a certain amount of explanatory comment but this could be expanded further.

The answer scores well on AO1 (knowledge and understanding) with the identification of more than 8 of the bullet points listed in the mark scheme.

(These are indicated in the text as *[1]*, *[2]* etc.) Clearly the candidate has a sound grasp of the topic, although the answer is probably stronger on the 'arguments for' section. All 8 marks were awarded.

For AO2 the answer has touched on each of the three sections. Paragraph 1 concerns the place of Christianity in British tradition and culture; paragraph 2 deals with the use of religion to create an integrated society; paragraph 3 argues that Christianity/religion is no longer relevant; paragraph 4 raises the issue of other religions; paragraph 5 compares religion with other aspects of the curriculum. Altogether this answer is worth 5 or 6 out of the 8 marks available for AO2. The mark might have been higher if there had been more obvious evaluation of the issues raised. The conclusion does arise from the reasons and arguments presented.

Communication is clear, coherent and relevant. There are a few careless spelling errors which restrict the answer to 3/4 AO4 marks.

Total marks 16/20

Sample question 2 (This question might appear in Unit 2)

> 'Artistic style' is a convenient term used to bring together works of art sharing similar characteristics. It is claimed that a new style develops when an artist (such as a painter, musician, writer, architect etc.) does something never done before. Another view is that art is constantly evolving in response to a variety of different factors.
>
> Identify different factors that may influence developments in art. Name an art form that you have studied and explain which factor contributed most to its development.

ANSWER

I am going to write about the development of art and in particular will consider Impressionism. Impressionism started in the late nineteenth century and had a big influence on many of the styles of painting that developed in the twentieth century.

Monet was the most important influence because he was the one who had the idea of doing impressionism. At first he painted in a traditional way in the studio. Someone gave him the idea of painting outdoors which he started to do. He liked using bright colours and had to paint very quickly before the light changed. He liked this new style of painting but most of the traditional painters did not. *[1]*

In Paris he made friends with other young painters who also didn't like the traditional way of painting and they began to experiment. *[6]* This made them unpopular with more experienced painters who wouldn't let them display their work in the Salon. They also criticised his method of using thick brush strokes. His work was criticised because it looked unfinished and simply gave an impression rather than a finished picture. This rejection encouraged him to ignore the art establishment in France and do things in his own way. He and some of his friends held their own exhibition and began to experiment with new ways of painting pictures. They broke the normally accepted rules of painting.

Another reason for the development of Impressionism was the invention of the camera. Up to this time most painters tried to make very realistic pictures. Photographs were much more accurate than they could paint and people began to go to photographers for their portraits rather than to a painter. As a result painters weren't able to make so much money and needed to find a different way of painting. *[10]*

Monet is the most famous name associated with Impressionism but he wasn't the only one to develop new ideas. He had a number of friends who also helped. These included Degas, Manet and Cezanne. They all had their own ideas which they contributed. This style was used earlier in England by Turner who probably influenced Monet.

Painting outdoors was a new technique and relied on new materials and equipment. Artists needed easily portable easels to take into the country. They also needed paint that would dry quickly in the open air. A most important development was the introduction of pre-mixed paints in lead tubes which they could take with them into the country. These developments at the end of the nineteenth century and so made the new style possible. *[10]*

Some of the painters wanted to explore different ideas and they weren't satisfied with just painting what was in front of them. Monet was particularly interested in the way that light kept on changing. A lot of his later pictures, especially those about water lilies were painted to explore this effect and were not intended at first to be sold.

At the time France was going through a difficult period. Once the greatest power in Europe they had just been humiliated in war by the Germans. *[3/8]* Some people wanted to resist change and get back to the good old days. Painters like this wanted to create pictures that celebrated historical successes rather than modern paintings which dealt with ordinary life. Others were prepared to experiment and look for new ways of doing things. Impressionist painters weren't interested in history and simply painted landscapes or pictures of ordinary people living ordinary lives. The political context encouraged the development of movements like Impressionism.

Impressionism developed for many different reasons, so you can't say it was the result of a single factor. I think the most important was the genius of one man Monet, who was prepared to develop his own ideas and ignore the criticism of experts who wanted him to conform to what they were doing. However if there hadn't been criticism he might never have changed his approach. In the same way if Impressionism hadn't become fashionable and copied by other painters we might never have heard of it and Monet would have been unknown. Similarly if there hadn't been new types of paint developed he wouldn't have been able to paint outside so easily. Impressionism, like most other new styles in painting or music developed because the right combination of influences existed at the same time.

MARK SCHEME

After marking the answer for AO1 and AO2, assess it for communication (AO4). The AO4 mark scheme is given on page 138.
AO1 (relevant knowledge and understanding) 8 marks
Identification of factors
Award 1 mark for each point, up to the maximum of 8 marks, such as:
1. originality of an individual artist

2. economic conditions
3. political circumstances
4. social conditions
5. religious and other beliefs
6. groups of artists working together
7. fashion and popular taste
8. key events (such as war or natural disaster)
9. changing attitudes in society
10. availability of new or different materials or technology
11. influence of earlier styles and/or artists.

AO2 (marshal evidence and draw conclusions) 8 marks
Award up to 4 marks for relevant arguments within each of the following areas, up to an overall maximum of 8 marks. Note that these arguments may link the development of the style to factors given above.

How different factors contributed to development E.g.:
• reaction against existing styles
• individuals associated with the style
• key characteristics of the style
• aspects of the development of the style
• key events associated with the style
• specific materials and technology that became available
• reaction to the new style of critics and/or supporters.

Evaluation of relative importance of different factors E.g.:
• no style is the result of a single factor
• there may be a trigger factor that is built on by other factors
• something new or different doesn't always lead to a new style
• clear identification with reasons of the key factor.

COMMENTARY

This candidate has virtually ignored the first part of the question, although it is possible to give some credit for points that are made which are relevant. The best approach would have been to give a list of different factors that could influence the development of any artistic style in any of the art forms. This would have been a quick way to accumulate a lot of marks for AO1 and would have provided a good basis for the second part of the answer.

Clearly the candidate has a good knowledge of the development of Impressionism and is able to identify some of the key influences on its origin and growth. However, the answer is more about Impressionism as an artistic style than about evaluating the various factors that contributed to its development.

There are probably 3 or 4 points that can be counted as sound AO1 points related to the first part of the question. (These are indicated in the text as *[1]*, *[2]* etc.) The answer is more successful in addressing the second part of the question: it would gain 3 marks for the development of the style plus another 3 or 4 marks for the evaluation.

The answer is clearly and coherently written. There are few spelling or grammatical errors. The candidate would have achieved all 4 AO4 marks if there had been a clear attempt to deal with the first part of the question. However, because there is a lack of relevance in the answer it only received 3 marks.

Total marks 10/20

Examiners' Tips

You must read this question carefully to recognise the two distinct parts of the question. Unless indicated, there is no transfer of marks between sections.

Practice question (This could appear in Unit 2)

This is a question for you to try on your own. Below it are some points that you could include. A mark scheme can be found on pages 158–9. Again there are 8 marks for AO1, 8 marks for AO2 and 4 marks for AO4.

Here are some key findings in a government report from 2006:

- The weekly median total individual income for all women in 2004/05 was 55 per cent of that of all men.
- Weekly median total individual income for women relative to men was lowest for women in pensioner couples: at 39 per cent of comparable men.
- Around 30 per cent of women had total, net and disposable individual incomes of less than £100 per week, more than twice the proportion of men.
- 38 per cent of men had total individual incomes of more than £400 per week compared with 15 per cent of women.
- Women's total individual incomes have risen in real terms by more than twice that of men's between 1996/97 and 2004/05.

Source: Individual income distribution by gender and family types, Women and equality unit, Department for Work and Pensions, 2006

'Attempts to bring about greater gender equality have been totally unsuccessful.'

Using your own knowledge as well as the information contained above, critically examine this opinion.

Some questions that you need to ask
- What do you understand by gender equality?
- What legislation has been introduced to bring about gender equality? (Note: it is appropriate to use information relating to approximately the last 50 years.)
- How should success or lack of success be measured?
- What conclusions can be drawn from the given information?
- What evidence is there to support the idea of success or failure?
- What factors might create practical barriers to greater equality?
- How do religion, different cultural values and traditions affect gender equality?

Some points to remember
- Do not confuse gender equality with other aspects of equality.
- You must be able to support what you say with evidence.
- The question statement does not refer to total equality but 'greater' equality. Is this significant?
- There may be areas where equality imbalance is in favour of women rather than men.
- You should be able to identify legislation concerning gender equality.
- Use evidence other than work and income, for example educational opportunity and achievement; age expectation; maternity and paternity rights.

Early legislation you might consider
1967 Abortion Act
1969 Divorce reform
1970 Equal Pay Act
1975 Sex Discrimination Act
1975 EU Equal Pay Act
1976 Domestic Violence and Matrimonial Procedures Act

> **Examiners' Tips**
>
> You are asked to critically examine this statement: it is not enough simply to describe gender equality. You should consider how accurate the assessment in the statement is. A clue is given in the use of the word 'totally'. Note also the use of the qualification 'greater'.

AO4 mark scheme (This is common to all pieces of extended writing)

Mark	Descriptor
	AO4: Communicate clearly and accurately in a concise, logical and relevant way. *The AO4 marks are not dependent upon the AO1 and AO2 marks.*
0	The answer is badly expressed or fails to treat the question seriously, there are many serious lapses in grammar and spelling or there is too little of the candidate's own writing to assess reliably.
1	The answer is only understandable in parts and may be irrelevant, writing may be in an inappropriate form, arguments are not clearly expressed, and in places grammar and spelling inhibit communication.
2	The answer is generally understandable, writing is often in the correct form. Arguments are sometimes coherent and relevant and grammar and spelling do not seriously inhibit communication.
3	The answer is broadly understandable, writing is in the correct form. Arguments are on the whole coherent and relevant, and grammar and spelling do not inhibit communication.
4	The answer is clear and lucid (writing in correct form is taken as a matter of course), arguments are coherent, well laid out and relevant, and there are few grammatical or spelling errors.

Further practice questions

Here are some other essay questions you might like to practise (page 139). You don't need to write them out as fully written answers. You might find this grid helpful in constructing skeleton answers.

Essay title:	
Analyse the question (what are you being asked to do?)	
Relevant evidence: 1. 2. 3. 4.	5. 6. 7. 8.
Arguments for: 1. 2. 3.	**Arguments against:** 1. 2. 3.
Evaluation of arguments:	
Conclusion:	

1. Explain 'artistic style'. Outline factors which contribute to the development of a new artistic style, illustrating your answer with reference to at least one artistic style.

2. What are the similarities and differences between creativity and innovation? Identify one innovative work of art that you have studied and explain why it is innovative.

3. Outline the similarities and differences between **two** different artistic styles.

4. 'Good art will always challenge the values of society.' Can this view be justified?

5. 'Conceptual art, like Tracey Emin's 'My bed', is not really art, it is merely a confidence trick on the public.' Using this, or other examples of conceptual or performance art, examine what is 'art'.

6. Should the arts have a purpose or should art exist for its own sake?

7. Does it matter if an artist's work causes offence to others provided it is true to the artist's own creative imagination?

8. Do you agree that bias is an essential feature of a free press in a democratic society?

9. Examine the view that the media do not create moral panics but merely report what is happening in society.

10. At present the government has too much control over media output.
    a. Explain how media output is controlled by government legislation today.
    b. Is this control necessary or desirable?

11. 'Soap operas fulfil a vitally important role in educating as well as entertaining viewers.' Do you agree? Illustrate your answer with reference to stories carried in current soap operas on television.

12. Examine the view that the Internet has reduced the role and influence of editors in selecting and shaping the news agenda.

Glossary of key terms

This glossary contains many of the key terms you will be expected to know and understand for your General Studies exam.

ABCs (Acceptable Behaviour Contracts) written agreements between a young person, the local housing office or Registered Social Landlord (RSL) and the local police in which the person agrees not to carry out a series of identifiable behaviours which have been defined as antisocial. The contracts are primarily aimed at young people aged between 10 and 18.

additional member system voting system used in Welsh Assembly and Scottish Parliament elections in which some members are elected in first past the post elections in single constituencies and then additional members are chosen for a group of constituencies to make each party's number of seats reasonably proportional to the party's share of the vote.

age certificate a means of categorising films with regard to their suitability for children and/or adults in terms of issues such as sex, violence, drugs, profanity or other types of mature content. Since 1982 video recordings have had similar certification.

alienation an individual's feelings of isolation or separation from a situation, group or culture.

alternative vote voting system in single member elections where voters indicate their order of preference between candidates (thus 1 – 2 – 3). The votes for the least successful candidate can be transferred to the second or next preference until one candidate has 50% or more votes.

arts (the) a broad subdivision of culture, composed of many expressive and creative activities. It is broader than 'art', which usually means the visual arts (comprising fine art, decorative art and crafts). 'The arts' include visual arts, performing arts, language arts, culinary arts and physical arts. It can refer to subjects of study concerned mainly with human creativity and social life.

ASBO (anti-social behaviour order) a means to control individuals whose behaviour disturbs, annoys or frightens others. These orders may restrict places a person may go and set times when they must stay at home. Breaking the terms of an ASBO can result in imprisonment.

assault a violent attack using physical weapons which threatens physical harm; an apparently violent attempt or threat to harm another person; a threat or show of force that causes a reasonable fear of an actual physical contact. **Assault and battery** is when a threat is accompanied by physical contact.

asylum a place of safety offering shelter or protection from physical danger; a place of protection or restraint for one or more classes of the disadvantaged, especially the mentally ill; the protection granted by a state to someone who has left their native country as a political refugee.

asylum seekers people who have left their own country and sought safety and protection in another because of the fear of persecution or physical violence.

attorney a person, typically a lawyer, appointed to act for another in legal matters. An 'attorney-in-fact' is an agent (who does not need to be licensed in law) who acts on behalf of another person, typically with respect to business, property or personal matters. An 'attorney-at-law', or lawyer, is a person trained and licensed to practise law by representing clients in legal matters and giving legal advice.

authoritarian a person or system favouring or enforcing strict obedience to authority at the expense of personal freedom. Often applied to totalitarian forms of government where oppressive measures are used to enforce obedience to the authority of the state. Usually an authoritarian government is undemocratic and has the power to govern without the consent of those who are governed.

Baroque a Western cultural period, commencing roughly at the turn of the 17th century. It was characterised by extravagance, drama, ornate detail and grandeur in sculpture, painting, literature, dance and music. In music, the term Baroque applies to the period c.1680–1740.

barrister a lawyer who often only becomes involved in a case in order to speak on behalf of a client in court. Barristers are engaged by solicitors to provide specialist advice on points of law but are rarely instructed directly by clients. A barrister is not an attorney and is forbidden, both by law and by professional rules, from conducting litigation, which is the role of a solicitor.

belief(s) the mental acceptance that something exists or is true, especially when there is a lack of proof; a firmly held opinion or conviction, especially religious or moral.

bias an inclination or prejudice for or against a thing or person.

blue-collar crime (sometimes **working-class crime**) any crime committed by an individual from a lower social class, as opposed to white-collar crime which is associated with crime committed by individuals of a higher social class. Usually refers to crimes such as burglary which depend more on opportunity than on the skill of the individual. May often involve the use of force and more likely to be reported to the police. See also **white-collar crime**.

blues a generally melancholic vocal and instrumental form of music based on the use of 'blue notes'. It emerged in African-American communities of the United States from spirituals, work songs, field hollers, shouts and chants, and rhymed simple narrative ballads. It demonstrates features characteristic of African music. Blues has influenced later American and Western popular music, as it formed the roots of jazz, rhythm and blues, rock and roll, hip-hop and other popular music forms.

BNP (British National Party) formed in 1982, a political party with some support in mainly poor urban working-class areas; it won less than 1% of the vote in the 2005 general election and is 'committed to stemming and reversing the tide of non-white immigration and to restoring, by legal changes, negotiation and consent the overwhelmingly white makeup of the British population that existed in Britain prior to 1948', proposing what it calls 'firm but voluntary incentives for immigrants and their descendants to return home'.

Booker (prize) see **Man Booker (prize)**.

British Commonwealth see **Commonwealth of Nations**.

British Empire the largest empire which ever existed, comprising colonies and subject nations run by Britain in all parts of the world as a result of discoveries by explorers and the development of trade; for a time it was the foremost global power, embracing about a quarter of the world's population in the 1920s; it has subsequently changed into the Commonwealth of Nations.

British National Party see **BNP**.

burglary (also called **breaking and entering** or **housebreaking**) a crime the essence of which is illegal entry into a building for the purposes of committing an offence, usually theft.

by-election an election held to replace an MP or member of a council who has died or resigned before the end of the term of office for which the person had been elected.

capital punishment the legally authorised killing of somebody as punishment for a crime. Crimes subject to capital punishment were sometimes called capital crimes.

case law a law or system of laws based on judicial precedent or the outcome of earlier cases rather than on statutory laws created by legislation.

censor an official who examines material that is to be published and suppresses parts considered to be offensive, harmful, objectionable or a threat to public security.

censorship the act of using state or group power to control freedom of expression, such as passing laws to prevent media from being published or propagated.

characteristic distinguishing feature of a person or object; feature or quality typical of a person, place or thing.

citizenship a legal relationship that a citizen has with a state. Living in a society such as the UK gives us both rights and responsibilities, so individuals and their property are protected by laws and courts; we also have responsibilities to treat each other in a civil manner, to share society's values and to obey the laws.

civil law law dealing with ordinary citizens (to be distinguished from criminal law). In civil law there is the attempt to right a wrong, honour an agreement or settle a dispute. If there is a victim, they get compensation, and the person who is the cause of the wrong pays (this is a civilised form of, or legal alternative to, revenge).

civil liberties freedoms which protect individuals from state abuse or government power. Civil liberties set limits for government so that it cannot abuse its power and interfere with the lives of its citizens, who typically enjoy rights such as freedom of association, freedom of assembly, freedom of religion, freedom of speech, the right to due process, to fair trial, to own property and to privacy.

civil partnership the legal recognition of same-sex relationships. Civil partnerships in the UK arose from the Civil Partnership Act 2004, which gave same-sex couples rights and responsibilities identical to civil marriage, i.e. civil partners have the same property rights as married couples from opposite sexes, the same exemption as married couples on inheritance tax, social security and pension benefits, and each is able to get parental responsibility for a partner's children.

class solidarity a Marxist concept involving the recognition by members of a particular class that they have shared interests with others involving a common identity or loyalty.

classical style artistic style associated with new styles which developed in the mid-18th century in architecture, literature and the arts. It emphasised order and hierarchy and favoured clear divisions between parts, brighter contrasts and colours and simplicity rather than complexity. In architecture and sculpture particularly it followed the style of ancient Greece and Rome.

coalition government government with ministers from two or more political parties, likely to occur if no one political party has a majority of MPs or at times of war when it is important to emphasise national unity (e.g. during the Second World War).

code a systematic collection of laws, rules or statutes; a set of conventions which govern behaviour or activity in a specific area of life.

cohabitation 'living together' in an intimate relationship which is both emotional and physical; there will usually be a common living place but the relationship exists without legal or religious sanction.

commercial pressure the effect of market forces which influence behaviour or shape output with a view to increasing profit or sales or obtaining a greater share of a market or encouraging spending.

common law a law or system of laws derived from custom or based on judicial precedent rather than statute or written laws.

Commonwealth of Nations a free association of independent states, most of which were once colonies or subject nations within the British Empire; formerly known as the Commonwealth of Nations, it now has 53 member countries including the UK.

community a social group with shared interests and often (but not necessarily) the same geographical location; if we speak of a 'bird watching community' or a 'stamp collecting community' it is the shared interest rather than the location which is the key factor.

commuting the process of travelling between where the individual commuter lives and a place of work; it happens mainly in industrialised societies, where cars, trains, buses and bicycles enable people to live far from their workplace.

compensation something awarded to make up for, balance or reduce the undesirable effects of loss, suffering or injury; something that makes up for an undesirable state of affairs; the action or process of compensating.

conceptual art art in which the concept or idea involved in the work is the most important aspect of the task. All planning and decisions are taken before a work is created and the execution of the work is mechanical. The transmission of ideas is more important than the creation of an art object.

congestion abnormal accumulation of vehicles on a particular road system causing delays and often, through exhaust fumes, high levels of air pollution.

congestion charge charge for driving on a particular road where there is a serious danger of congestion arising; such charges are applied to reduce traffic in cities such as London and Durham.

consequentialism a form of moral reasoning which assumes that the consequences of an act are the moral basis for judging the act. See also utilitarianism.

Conservative right-wing political party which favours private enterprise, low taxation and service delivery via the private sector; it gains strong support in rural and suburban England but is much weaker in northern urban areas, Scotland, Wales and Northern Ireland. The party is the successor of the Tory party which existed in the 18th and 19th centuries. In contemporary times, it is divided over Europe though generally more Eurosceptic than other UK parties apart from UKIP.

conspiracy a secret agreement or act of two or more persons to obtain some goal, to do something harmful or to break a law at some time in the future.

constitution a system of rules and procedures for governing an institution, which can be a country or any other political organisation.

contemporary living, occurring or originating at the same time; belonging to or occurring in the present; modern in style or design.

content (in aesthetics or art appreciation) a key means by which a work of art affects an audience and expresses the creator's purpose. It includes not only the 'story' contained in the work but also the 'message', moral content or comment on the human condition.

copyright the exclusive legal right given to the originator for a fixed number of years to exploit (publish, copy or distribute) a piece of work (usually literary, artistic or musical).

corporal punishment the deliberate infliction of pain as a form of physical punishment such as beating, whipping, branding or mutilating. Once a common form of punishment it is now outlawed, especially with regard to children, in Europe and in many other parts of the world.

credit card plastic card on which the owner can pay for goods by automatic borrowing; typically the credit card company makes a profit on the transaction both by charging the shopkeeper and also charging the shopper interest for any monies not repaid at the end of the month.

criminal law the area of law pertaining to crime and punishment; a system of law concerned with the punishment of offenders. It is typically enforced by government rather than by individuals.

criteria (singular **criterion**) a standard, principle or test by which individual things or people may be compared and judged or decided.

crossbench peer (or **crossbencher**) a member of the House of Lords who has not declared a political allegiance or joined a political party.

crown court a court of criminal jurisdiction which deals with serious offences and with appeals referred from a magistrates' court.

culture attitudes, norms, values, loyalties and beliefs prevalent in a society, including icons of symbolic importance (e.g. Stonehenge as a symbol of historic traditions); often sub-cultures arise where particular sets of individuals develop different loyalties, values or lifestyles.

DA notice an official request to news editors not to publish or broadcast items on specified subjects. They provide advice and guidance to the media about defence and counter-terrorist information the publication of which could damage national security. They are voluntary and not legally enforceable: the final authority for deciding whether or not to publish rests with news editors or publishers.

damages a sum of money claimed or awarded in compensation for loss or injury; money awarded to the claimant in a civil action.

debit card a plastic card like a credit card, but it takes money directly from the bank account rather than borrowing money at a rate of interest.

deduction a form of reasoning in which if the premises are true, and the logic is good, then the conclusion must be true. See also **induction**.

deflation a decrease in the general level of prices, i.e. in the nominal cost of goods and services as well as wages.

delegate a person sent or authorised to represent others, in particular a representative sent to a conference; a member of a committee; to authorise someone to act as a representative; to commit a task to someone, especially a subordinate.

demand a desire to purchase goods and services backed up by an ability to do so. Prices usually rise if demand exceeds supply and fall if supply exceeds demand. See also **supply**.

Democratic Unionist Party (DUP) political party which operates in Northern Ireland where it fiercely asserts the rights, beliefs and interests of Protestants. The DUP was the largest party in the Northern Ireland power-sharing government in 2008.

deterrent a thing or action that discourages or is intended to discourage someone from doing something.

deviant a person whose behaviour diverges from usual or accepted standards, especially in sexual or social terms.

devolution the transfer of some powers, and the delegation of some functions, from a sovereign government to a different tier of government, e.g. from government offices in Whitehall and the Westminster Parliament to the Scottish Executive and Parliament and the Welsh Executive and Welsh Assembly.

digital relating to or using signals or information represented as digits (numbers from 0 to 9); characterised by electronic and especially computerised technology.

discrimination, negative unfavourable treatment based on prejudice especially regarding race, age or sex.

discrimination, positive favourable treatment designed to overcome prejudice, e.g. an employer might restrict the shortlist for job interviews to candidates with attributes currently under-represented in the firm.

dispersal order a power issued under the Anti-Social Behaviour Act 2003 which allows a senior police officer, with the agreement of the local authority, to designate an area where there is persistent anti-social behaviour. The power allows police officers to disperse groups of two or more, making them move out of the area, especially those who are responsible for (existing or future) vandalism in the area. After 9pm it can be used to return young people under 16 to their home address.

diversity the recognition that in a modern multicultural society many people will participate from different ethnic, religious and social backgrounds with a wide variety of experiences which are to be celebrated and regarded as a strength.

divorce the ending of a marriage before the death of either spouse; recognition of divorce is resisted by various religions, particularly Muslims and Roman Catholics, with the latter believing that marriage vows once taken are permanent and cannot be erased, so in the eyes of this church re-marriage is not permitted.

DNA (deoxyribonucleic acid) an acid which contains the genetic instructions used in the development and functioning of all known living organisms. The main role of DNA molecules is the long-term storage of information. DNA is often compared to a set of blueprints, since it contains instructions needed to construct other components of cells such as proteins.

dome a rounded vault forming the roof of a building or structure; a structural element of architecture which resembles the hollow upper half of a sphere.

DUP see **Democratic Unionist Party**.

dystopia an imaginary place or society in which everything is bad, often characterised by human suffering and misery. See also **utopia**.

editor a person who is in charge of a newspaper, magazine or multi-author book; a person who commissions or prepares written or recorded material; a person who prepares (as in literary material) for publication or public presentation; assembles (as with a moving picture or tape recording) by cutting and rearranging; or alters, adapts or refines to bring about conformity to a standard or to suit a particular purpose.

Electoral Commission a body established by Parliament in 2000 to (i) advise government on the reform of electoral law, (ii) help determine the boundaries of council wards and divisions, (iii) decide the procedures for referendums, (iv) ensure that all elections are conducted fairly, (v) regulate political parties and the funding of political campaigns, (vi) promote public awareness of electoral systems used in the UK.

electoral reform changing the voting system, often (but not always) from a first past the post system to a system of proportional representation.

electorate all those who are entitled to vote and listed on an electoral register within the UK.

elitism the belief that those who are members of an elite – people with outstanding personal abilities, intellect, wealth, privileged education or other distinctive attributes – are those whose views on a matter should be taken the most seriously or carry the most weight. Pluralists and egalitarians are critical of elitism, seeing it as a concentration of power into the hands of a tiny and untypical minority.

emigration the act of moving out of a country.

emotion a strong feeling, such as joy, anger or sadness; an instinctive or intuitive feeling as distinct from reasoning or knowledge; a person's internal state of being and involuntary, subjective, physiological response to an object or a situation, based in or tied to physical state and sensory feelings.

environment in a social sense, the culture that an individual lives in, and the people and institutions with whom they interact.

equal opportunities an approach where a social environment is created in which people are not excluded from the activities of society, such as education, employment, human rights or health care, on the basis of individual characteristics such as age, sex, size, ethnicity or any disabilities.

equality a social state of affairs in which all people have the same status and equal rights before the law, at the very least in voting rights, freedom of speech and assembly, property rights and access to education, health care and other forms of social security; however, many people for reasons such as poverty or inadequate education or lack of confidence may not have the capacity to exercise and benefit fully from such rights.

ethics a branch of philosophy dealing with the good life and good conduct.

ethnic minority a person or group of people who have a different culture, religion or language to the main one in the place or country where they live. Inevitably any large multicultural society contains ethnic minorities, often including many people speaking different languages with different ethnicities. They may have migrated to the society or be the descendents of those who came as migrants. In some places, there may no longer be a single ethnic majority group.

ethnicity a group of human beings whose members identify with each other, usually on the basis of a presumed common genealogy or ancestry. Ethnic identity can also be marked by the recognition from others of a group's distinctiveness and by common cultural, linguistic, religious, behavioural or biological characteristics.

EU Commission the EU's executive, responsible for initiating legislation and the day-to-day working of the EU. It is currently composed of 27 commissioners, one from each member state. The President of the Commission and all the other commissioners are nominated by the Council. Appointment of the Commission President, and also the Commission itself, must be confirmed by Parliament.

EU Council of Ministers the body that forms the main part of the EU's legislature. It is composed of the national ministers responsible for the policy area being addressed (so the chancellor of the exchequer and other finance ministers would attend when the Council of Ministers was dealing with finance, but the transport minister when transport was the topic to be considered). In addition to legislation, the Council also exercises executive functions in relation to the Common Foreign and Security Policy.

EU Court of Justice the body that interprets and applies the treaties and the law of the EU. The Court of Justice mainly deals with cases brought by member states, the EU institutions and cases referred to the EU's courts by the courts in member states. These courts are not to be confused with the European Court of Human Rights which operates under the aegis of the Council of Europe (not part of the EU).

European Convention on Human Rights agreement promoted by the Council of Europe (not the EU) and enforced by the European Court of Human Rights in Strasbourg; the convention was incorporated into UK law as the Human Rights Act 1998, allowing complainants to apply to UK courts rather than having to go to the Strasbourg court.

European Parliament body that deals with legislative work not undertaken by the Council of Ministers. The 785 Members of the European Parliament (MEPs) are directly elected by EU voters every five years. Although MEPs are elected on a national basis, they sit according to political groups rather than their nationality, e.g. all the Socialists including Labour MEPs from the UK sit together. Each country has a set number of seats: the UK has 78. The Parliament also has the power to reject or censure the Commission. The President of the European Parliament carries out the role of speaker in Parliament and represents it externally.

European Union (EU) alliance of 27 countries including the UK originating from the original Treaty of Rome 1957 when France, West Germany, Italy, Belgium, the Netherlands and Luxembourg formed the European Economic Community; Britain and Ireland joined in 1973.

exports goods and services sold or given to other countries.

family, extended a wider family unit common in the 19th century typically involving parents and children as well as other close relatives all living in relatively close proximity to each other.

family, nuclear a close family unit common in the 20th century typically involving mother, father and an average of two children. In the 21st century there is a minority of nuclear families: many married couples live together without children or have children but are content to cohabit and not get married; many more single people live on their own without a long-standing relationship.

fine a sum of money exacted as a penalty by a court of law or other authority; to punish (by fining); a forfeiture or penalty paid to an injured party in a civil action.

first past the post system electoral system operating in single member constituencies in which the party with most votes wins the seat; if there are a number of candidates the percentage vote obtained by the winning candidate may be well under 50%, sometimes even under 30%.

floating voter voter who is not strongly committed to supporting any one political party and may change the party they support from election to election.

'folk devil' a person or thing held to be a bad influence on society. Folk devils are portrayed in the media as outsiders and deviants who are blamed for crimes or other social problems (see **moral panics**). The mass media sometimes attempt to create new folk devils to create controversies. Sometimes such campaigns can influence national politics and legislation.

forgery a fraudulent copy or imitation of a work of art or other object; the crime of fraudulently making or altering a writing or signature purporting to be made by another; false making or material alteration of an object with the purpose of deceit and fraud.

fraud wrongful or criminal act or deception intended to result in personal or financial gain; a person or thing intended to deceive; someone who is not what they pretend to be; an impostor.

freedom, negative (freedom from) as conceived by Isaiah Berlin, freedom that involves an absence of obstacles put in the way of an individual's action by other people.

freedom of information the right of access to information or records held by government bodies. The Freedom of Information Act 2000 is the implementation of freedom of information legislation in the United Kingdom on a national level.

freedom, positive (freedom to) as conceived by Isaiah Berlin, freedom that involves an individual's power to make free choices leading to action.

full employment the economic condition when everyone who wishes to work is employed. To most people, full employment means no unemployment, yet most economists state that it can mean an unemployment rate higher than 0%. For example, British economist William Beveridge stated that an unemployment rate of 3% was full employment.

garage music UK garage (also known as UKG) refers to several different varieties of modern electronic dance music generally connected to the evolution of house in the United Kingdom in the mid 1990s. New York house, also known as New York garage, US garage or just garage, is a style of house music born in the Paradise Garage nightclub in New York City, USA in the early 1980s. It should not to be confused with UK garage.

gene a unit made up of DNA within a chromosome; it may have a variety of functions, including determining a characteristic of an individual.

general election election when all seats in Parliament need to be filled; such elections must occur in the UK every five years, though typically general elections are usually held within about four years of the previous election on a date proposed by the Prime Minister to HM The Queen. Usually there are contests in all constituencies (650 at the next election expected in 2009 or 2010) and candidates must all be persons aged 18 or over and listed on an election register but not necessarily in the area for which they seek election.

giant evils see **welfare state**.

glass ceiling refers to situations where the progress of a qualified person, typically a woman, within the hierarchy of an organisation is halted at a particular level because of some form of discrimination, most commonly sexism or racism.

global warming the increase in the average temperature of the Earth's near-surface air and oceans in recent decades and its projected continuation. The global average air temperature near the Earth's surface rose 0.74 ± 0.18 °C (1.33 ± 0.32 °F) during the hundred years ending in 2005, leading the Intergovernmental Panel on Climate Change (IPCC) to conclude that 'most of the observed increase in globally averaged temperatures since the mid-twentieth century is very likely due to the observed increase in anthropogenic [man-made] greenhouse gas concentrations' via the greenhouse effect.

globalisation the development of an increasingly integrated global economy marked especially by free trade, free flow of capital and the tapping of cheaper foreign labour markets; the process of increasing interconnectedness in the world; the process of making a world economy dominated by capitalist models.

Gothic style a style of architecture prevalent in western Europe in the 12th to 16th centuries characterised by the converging of weights and strains at isolated points upon slender vertical piers and counterbalancing buttresses and by pointed arches and vaulting.

Gothick a romanticised revival of the Gothic style of architecture popular in 18th and 19th centuries; a genre of novel popular in the 18th and 19th centuries characterised by an atmosphere of mystery and horror using desolate or remote settings and involving macabre, mysterious or violent incidents.

Green Party the main green political party in England and Wales. It is unrepresented in the House of Commons, but has one life peer within the House of Lords and a handful of members have been elected to the European Parliament, the Scottish Parliament, the London Assembly and in local government.

hereditary peer a person who holds a peerage which could be inherited from a parent or, on death, inherited by a son or daughter; only 92 hereditary peers continue to have places in the House of Lords.

hip hop music a genre of popular music of US black and hispanic origin typically consisting of a rhythmic style of speaking called rap over electronic backing beats performed on a turntable by a DJ. The term rap is sometimes used synonymously with hip hop music, though it originally referred only to rapping itself. Beats are traditionally sampled from portions of other songs by a DJ. Live bands are also used, especially in newer music. Many instrumental acts are also defined as hip hop.

homicide the killing of one human being by another whether premeditated or unintentional; murder.

homophobia term used to describe the irrational fear of, aversion to or discrimination against homosexuals.

House of Commons the lower house of the UK Parliament.

House of Lords the upper house of the UK Parliament.

household defined by the Office for National Statistics as 'one person or a group of people who have the accommodation as their only or main residence and, for a group, either share at least one meal a day or share the living accommodation, that is, a living room or sitting room'.

human anatomy the branch of medicine and biology concerned with (human) bodily structure, especially as revealed by dissection; the bodily structure of a person, animal or plant.

human rights a right or entitlement (such as freedom from unlawful imprisonment, torture and execution) regarded as belonging fundamentally, justifiably and intrinsically to every person.

humanism a rationalistic outlook or system of thought attaching prime importance to human rather than divine or supernatural matters; a renaissance cultural movement which turned away from medieval scholasticism and revived interest in ancient Greek and Roman thought; a secular ethical system that centres on humans, especially the values, needs, interests, abilities, dignity and freedom of human beings.

humanist a person who believes in or practises a doctrine, attitude or way of life centred on human interests or values; a philosophy that rejects supernaturalism and stresses an individual's dignity, worth and capacity for self-realisation through reason.

hung parliament a term that refers to a Parliament in which one party has fewer than half the members, meaning that there would be a minority government or coalition.

hypothesis (scientific) a possible explanation, based on observation, for a phenomenon or set of phenomena. It is used in science to design experiments to test the explanation. See also **theory (scientific)**.

identity the way individuals label themselves as members of particular groups (e.g. English or Irish, working class or middle class, black or white, male or female).

ideology an organised collection of ideas, i.e. a comprehensive vision, as a way of looking at things; examples could be conservativism (tendency to support the status quo), liberalism (belief in individualism) or socialism (tendency to an egalitarian point of view).

immigration the act of moving into a country.

imports goods or services purchased from other countries.

impressionism a style or movement in painting characterised by a concern with depicting the visual impression of the moment and using visible brush strokes, ordinary subject matters and an emphasis on the changing qualities of light; a literary or artistic style that used imagery and symbolism to portray a feeling or experience rather than to achieve an accurate depiction; a style of musical composition in which traditional harmony was less important than harmonic effects as a way of conveying the composers' impressions. The style is associated with the period c.1870 to 1900.

incapacitate to deprive of capacity or natural power; disable; prevent from functioning in a normal way; deprive of legal capacity.

indictable rendering a person who commits an offence liable to be charged with a serious crime that warrants trial by jury.

indictment a formal charge or accusation of a serious crime; an official written accusation on behalf of the government for a serious offence; a document outlining serious charges of an accused.

induction a form of reasoning which reaches conclusions by using a few observations to make a generalisation. Although the conclusion can be a good one, it is not necessarily so, because not all possible observations can be made.

inflation an increase in the general level of prices, which means that the nominal cost of goods and services as well as wages will rise.

installation art a genre of art which usually consists of multiple components often in mixed media, including the physical features of a site, to create a conceptual experience in a particular environment. It is usually exhibited in a large space in an arrangement specified by the artist and it is concerned with the way a particular space is experienced. Some installations are site-specific in that they are designed to only exist in the space for which they were created.

institution an organisation founded for a specific purpose (often educational, public service, cultural or social); an official organisation with an important role in a state; a custom or practice of a society or culture.

interactive responding to the user; allowing a two-way flow of information between an electronic device and a user; involving the actions or input of a user; relating to, or being a two-way electronic communication system (such as a telephone, cable television or a computer) that involves a user's orders (such as for information or merchandise) or responses (such as to a poll).

interest the money we have to pay if we borrow money on a credit card, a personal loan or a mortgage; the payment we receive from a bank or building society for depositing savings with them. Generally the rate we receive for saving with a bank is less than the rate borrowers are charged; this is how banks and similar financial institutions aim to achieve a profit on operations.

investment economists believe that when a firm buys a new efficient machine to improve productivity, this is capital investment: the firm is hoping the machine will help it to cut costs and make money; equally if a financial adviser encourages an investor to put his money into the shares of a particular company, this is also regarded as an investment: in this case the investor will hope the shares purchased go up in value (capital gain) and that the firm will declare good dividends (i.e. the investor's share of the profits from the company).

147

judge public officer appointed to try cases in a court of law; a public official whose duty is to administer the law, especially by presiding over trials and giving judgements; one who carefully weighs evidence and tests a premise; to sit in judgment to determine or pronounce after inquiry and deliberation; a person qualified and able to give a decision.

jury a body of people (typically 12 in the UK) chosen from the general population and sworn to give a verdict on the basis of evidence submitted in court.

justice a magistrate or judge appointed to administer and maintain the law.

Justice of the Peace (JP) a lay magistrate appointed to hear and administer summary justice in minor cases and to commit to trial in the Crown Court.

label a classifying name given to a person (especially inaccurately) to attach them to a particular social group; to assign to a category. Labelling means defining or describing a person in terms of behaviour, e.g. describing someone who has broken a law as a criminal.

labelling theory (or **social reaction theory**) theory concerned with how the self-identity and behaviour of an individual is influenced (or created) by how that individual is categorised and described by others in their society. The theory focuses on the linguistic tendency of majorities to negatively label minorities or those seen as deviant from norms, and is associated with the concept of a self-fulfilling prophecy and stereotyping.

Labour centre left party in the UK. Founded in the early 20th century, it has been the principal alternative to the Conservatives in England, Scotland and Wales since the 1920s but not in Northern Ireland, where the SDLP occupies a similar position on the political spectrum. Labour is firmly committed to the Atlantic alliance with the USA although the war in Iraq is not popular in the UK; Labour is also broadly pro-Europe and aims to reduce social exclusion and inequality.

legislation the process of passing laws.

legislature a governmental body with the power to make, amend or repeal laws; a body of persons having the power to legislate; an organised body having the authority to make laws for a political unit. In the UK Parliament is the legislature.

Liberal Democrats a liberal political party in the UK formed in 1988 by the merger of the Liberal Party and the Social Democratic Party. The Liberal Democrats are the third largest party in the UK Parliament, with 63 MPs in March 2008 (compared with the six MPs the Liberals

had for much of the 1950s), favouring a commitment to social justice, the welfare state, economic freedom, competitive markets and environmentalist 'make polluters pay' values; the party opposed British participation in the war in Iraq and are considered the most pro-European party in British politics.

life chances the opportunities each individual has to improve their quality of life.

life expectancy the average number of years a human has before death, conventionally calculated from the time of birth, but also can be calculated from any specified age; life expectancy is affected by factors such as infant mortality, nutrition, public health, poverty and access to health care. Typically life expectancy in the UK is higher for women than men; a 65 year old female today could expect to live for about 20 years more (to 85) while a 65 year old man could expect to survive for another 17 years. Those living in affluent areas in the UK can expect to live up to 15 years longer than those living in deprived urban areas.

literature written works, especially those regarded as having artistic merit; writings having excellence of form or expression and expressing ideas of permanent or universal interest; books and writings on a particular subject.

longevity having a long life; the quality of being long lasting; one of the measures used in aesthetic evaluation.

low cost carriers airlines that offer generally low fares in exchange for eliminating many traditional passenger services. The concept originated in the USA before spreading to Europe in the early 1990s and subsequently to much of the rest of the world.

magistrate (stipendiary) a Justice of the Peace; a judicial officer or lay judge with limited powers who administers the law; a justice who conducts a court concerned with minor offences and holds preliminary hearings into more serious ones.

magistrates' court court that has jurisdiction over minor civil and criminal cases; it may have jurisdiction in civil or criminal cases, or both. Most criminal cases start in the magistrates' courts where the less serious offences (over 95% of all cases) are handled entirely. The more serious offences are passed on to the Crown Court, to be dealt with by a judge and jury.

Man Booker (prize) a literary prize awarded each year for the best original full-length novel, written in the English language, by a citizen of either the Commonwealth of Nations or the Republic of Ireland.

mandate a duty or permission to carry out the policies in the manifesto of a winning party if they subsequently become the government.

manifesto the policy statement issued by a candidate or political party prior to a general election.

Mannerism excessive or self-conscious use of a distinctive ostentatious style in art, literature or music; a style of 16th century Italian art characterised by distortions in scale and perspective, excessive elongation of human figures and the use of bright, often lurid, colours.

manslaughter the crime of killing a human being unlawfully but without 'malice aforethought' (bad intention), or otherwise in circumstances not amounting to murder.

marginal seat a constituency in Parliament where the winning MP has a small majority, so there is a real possibility that another party may win the seat at a future election. In the 2005 election, examples of marginal seats were Romsey (LD maj over Con 125 [0.2%]), Warwick and Leamington (Lab maj over Con 266 [0.5%]) and Edinburgh South (Lab maj over LD 405 [1.0%]).

media bias the perception that news media report events in a manner that is not neutral. It describes a real or perceived bias of journalists and news producers within the mass media, in the selection of which events to report and how they are covered. Practical limitations to media neutrality include the inability of journalists to report all available stories and facts. Since it is impossible to report everything, some bias is inevitable.

meritocracy involves appointments being made and/or responsibilities given based on demonstrated ability (merit) and talent rather than through favouritism or other considerations such as wealth, family connections, class privilege, cronyism or other reflections of social position or political power.

Ministry of Justice a department of the UK government, reorganised from the Department for Constitutional Affairs and the Home Office in 2007. It has responsibility for sentencing policy, probation, prisons and prevention of re-offending in England and Wales. It administers some tribunals and has various functions, such as human rights and electoral reform, throughout the whole of the UK.

modern of or relating to the present or recent times; characterised by or using the most-up-to-date techniques or equipment; a recent style in art, architecture and music; contemporary.

Modernism modern ideas, methods or styles; a movement in the arts that aims to break with traditional forms or ideas and search for new forms of expression; a tendency in theology to accommodate traditional religious teaching to contemporary thought and especially to devalue supernatural elements; a religious movement in the early 20th century that tried to reconcile Roman Catholic dogma with modern science and philosophy; any of several styles of art, architecture, literature etc. that flourished in the 20th century.

monocultural society a society or state in which everyone shares the same cultural attributes; such a society or state is a distinct contrast to a multicultural society; the supposed desirability of a monocultural society could lead a fanatic such as Hitler to pursue a policy of ethnic cleansing through his Holocaust policy.

moral panic a semi-spontaneous or media-generated mass movement based on the perception that an individual, group, community or culture is dangerously deviant and poses a menace to society. See also **'folk devil'**.

morality distinguishing between good and bad, from which we derive moral reasoning; arguments designed to distinguish between good and bad.

mortgage an agreement between a property owner and a bank or building society or similar financial organisation to lend the property owner up to 100% of the value of the property to enable a purchase to be made, to be paid back with interest over an agreed number of years.

motorway a high capacity road designed to carry fast motor traffic safely. In the UK motorways are predominantly dual-carriageway roads, with two, three or four lanes in each direction, and all have grade-separated access.

multicultural society a society that embraces both cultural and ethnic diversity within the population of a particular social space. Multiculturalism aims for a society that extends equal status to distinct cultural and religious groups with no one culture predominating.

national income along with national output, a measure used in economics to estimate the value of goods and services produced in an economy. Economists use a system of national accounts including common measures such as Gross National Product (GNP) and Gross Domestic Product (GDP).

national insurance a system of taxes and related social security benefits in the UK first introduced in 1911. The tax component of the system consists of taxes paid by employees and employers on weekly earnings and other benefits-in-kind; the self-employed are taxed based upon profits. Such taxes are said to be National

Insurance Contributions (NICs) to provide some weekly income benefits and some lump sum benefits to participants upon death, retirement, unemployment, maternity or disability.

national minimum wage legal wage limit that took effect in the UK on 1 April 1999 and is increased each year. It is set at a different hourly rate for people under and over 22.

nationalisation the act of taking an industry or assets into the public ownership of a national government. Nationalisation usually refers to private assets, but may also mean assets owned by lower levels of government, such as councils. After 1945 the Labour government nationalised industries such as coal, steel, gas, telephones and electricity, most of which were privatised (sold to private shareholders) by the Conservatives in the 1980s.

NATO (North Atlantic Treaty Organisation) a military alliance established by the signing of the North Atlantic Treaty in 1949. With headquarters in Brussels, NATO established a system of collective defence whereby its member states agree to mutual defence in response to an attack by any external party. Since the end of the Cold War NATO has grown to 26 member countries.

naturalisation the process that gives to a citizen of another country resident in the UK all the rights enjoyed by a natural-born UK citizen.

nature within the nature–nurture debate, the 'nature' element is concerned with the relative importance of an individual's innate qualities (nature) in determining or causing individual differences in physical and behavioural traits.

nurture within the nature–nurture debate, the 'nurture' element is concerned with the relative importance of an individual's personal experiences (nurture) in determining or causing individual differences in physical and behavioural traits.

obscene offensive, rude, shocking or disgusting by accepted current standards of morality and decency; liable to deprave or corrupt; morally wrong.

opinion poll a survey of public opinion from a particular sample. Opinion polls are usually designed to discover the opinions of a population by asking a small number of people a series of questions and then extrapolating the answers to the larger group.

parliament in the UK the highest legislature consisting of the monarch and the Houses of Lords and Commons.

partisan identification a statistical measure indicating the extent to which an individual identifies with a particular political party; in general terms partisan identification has declined in recent years leading to apparently greater voter volatility.

party list system a voting system in which the voter indicates which party they wish to support; the party decides the order of preference of its candidates, so although the system leads to a proportional result, it takes away from the voter any influence over the individual(s) elected.

patent a government licence to an individual or body conferring a right or title for a fixed period of time; the sole right to make, use or sell an invention; a declaration issued by a government agency declaring someone the inventor of a new invention and having the privilege of stopping others from making, using or selling the claimed invention.

peer group a group of people probably with similar ages and interests, e.g. a group of friends. It may be an alternative source of influence within the socialisation process when compared to reference groups such as parents, teachers or managers.

pension, occupational a pension to which both employer (whether in public or private sector) and employee contribute which will be paid by or on behalf of the employer when the employee reaches retirement.

pension, private a pension paid by a pension provider such as Prudential or Standard Life to which an employee or the employer will have paid contributions over a worker's working lifetime; contributions to a private pension may have attracted tax relief for the employer and/or the employee but there is no other involvement on the part of the state or government.

pension, stakeholder a form of private pension introduced in 2001 in the UK to encourage more long-term saving for retirement, particularly among those on low to moderate earnings. Such pensions are required to meet conditions set out by government, i.e. a cap on charges, low minimum contributions and flexibility in stopping and starting contributions. All employers with five or more workers are required to offer a stakeholder pension scheme or a suitable alternative.

pension, state a pension paid by the UK government to men aged 65 and women aged 60 who have made national insurance contributions for a given number of years, although from 2010 the state pension age will start to be equalised and for women will rise, eventually reaching the age of 65 by 2020; by 2044 the retirement age for both men and women will have risen to 68, a reflection of longer life expectancy.

performance art a form of art in which the artist creates a live performance, often using a variety of media.

perspective the art of representing three-dimensional objects on a two-dimensional surface so as to convey the impression of height, depth, width and relative distance; a view or prospect; the way that objects appear smaller when they are further away and the way parallel lines appear to meet each other at a point in the distance.

philosophy from the Greek meaning 'love of wisdom', the study of how we should live, what exists, what is knowledge and the principles of reasoning.

Plaid Cymru the Party of Wales which elected its first MP in 1966; it favours the establishment of an independent Welsh state within the European Union. In 2007 it became coalition partner with Labour in the Welsh Executive. In March 2008 the party held three out of 40 seats in the UK Parliament and it also had 15 of 60 seats in the National Assembly for Wales.

pluralism as a contrast to elite theory, pluralists assert that political power in society does not lie with just the electorate but is distributed among a wide number of groups in society including the media, churches, interest groups, business and trade union organisations, voluntary groups and political parties.

Pop art art based on modern popular culture and the mass media, especially as a critical or ironic comment on traditional fine art values; started in the 1960s, Pop art uses images and objects from ordinary everyday life and often uses techniques from commercial art and advertising.

pornography printed or visual material intended explicitly to stimulate sexual excitement but which would be considered unpleasant or offensive by many people.

post-modernism a late 20th-century style and concept in the arts and architecture which represents a departure from modernism and has as a central theme a general distrust of theories and ideologies; a style which includes features from several different periods in the past or from the present and past.

pressure group an organised group of people who seek to influence political decisions and policy, without seeking election to public office. 'Insider' pressure groups have knowledge and expertise which the government wishes to share, so such groups have no difficulty in attracting the attention of government. 'Outsider' pressure groups wish to change the policy ends and/or means of the government so may have considerable difficulty in attracting

the attention of government; as a result such groups will organise petitions and hold rallies or demonstrations as well as aiming to influence the media and public opinion; rarely do governments heed the advice from an outsider group even though such groups are important components of a pluralist democracy.

price the price of a good or service is determined by the demand and supply for it. If demand in relation to supply is high (as in an auction) the price will tend to rise; if supply exceeds demand, the price will tend to fall.

private sector that part of the economy which is both run for profit and is not controlled by public bodies such as government departments, devolved governments or county, district or unitary councils.

probation the release of an offender from detention, subject to a period of good behaviour under supervision; a period of time when a criminal must behave well and not commit more crimes in order to avoid being sent to prison; a type of sentence where convicted criminals are allowed to continue living in the community but will automatically be sent to jail if they violate certain conditions.

proportional representation (PR) a type of voting system which aims to give political parties as nearly as possible the same proportion of places in Parliament as it receives votes (e.g. 51% seats only if 51% votes are received); PR systems include additional member system, party list system and single transferable vote system but not alternative vote or first past the post.

public expenditure expenditure by the public sector. See also **public sector**.

public sector part of the economic and administrative system that involves the delivery of goods and services by and for the government, whether national, regional or local.

punk a loud, fast-moving, aggressive and often offensive form of rock music popular in the late 1970s, known for short songs with electric guitars, strong drums and a direct, unproduced approach; a social and musical movement rooted in rebelling against the established order, popular among young people, especially in the late 1970s, expressed through shocking behaviour, clothes and hair, and fast, loud music.

racism a widely held belief by members of one race that they are inherently superior to people who belong to other races.

rap(ping) (also referred to as MCing or emceeing) a vocal style in which the performer speaks rhythmically and in rhyme, generally to a beat.

Rappers may perform poetry which they have written ahead of time, or improvise rhymes on the spot. Though rap is usually an integral component of hip hop music, DJs sometimes perform and record alone. See also **hip hop music**.

realism the representation of things in a way that is accurate and true to life.

reference group in contrast to a peer group (friends, contemporaries), a reference group is a sociological concept referring to another group such as parents, teachers, mentors or line managers in an employment situation by whose views and advice a person might be expected to be influenced.

regime a government, especially an authoritarian one; a system or method of government; the government in power.

regulation a law or administrative rule or directive made and maintained by an authority or organisation to guide or prescribe the conduct of members of that organisation.

regulatory bodies a group or organisation appointed by an authority to regulate or control a specific field of activity; an official or organisation who makes certain that the companies who operate a system, such as the national electricity supply, work effectively and fairly within the law.

rehabilitation the process of restoring to health or normal life by training and/or therapy, especially after imprisonment.

Renaissance the revival or rebirth of art, literature and ideas under the influence of classical models in the 14th–16th centuries.

representational relating to or denoting art which depicts the physical appearance of things; showing things as they are normally seen.

rights entitlements. There are two distinct ideas here: **natural rights** are a system of entitlements that are not open to human modification, such as the right to life; **legal rights** are decided by whatever judicial system operates in a particular society.

road pricing a method of charging to pay for a road to be constructed (tolls) or congestion charges, including those which vary by time of day, by the specific road or by the specific vehicle type being used. Road pricing has two distinct objectives: revenue generation, usually to finance road construction or maintenance, and congestion pricing for demand management purposes, e.g. London's congestion charge.

robbery the action of robbing a person (taking property unlawfully) by force or threat of force; larceny from the person or from the presence of a person by violence or threat; the crime of stealing.

rock ('n' roll) a type of popular dance music originating in the 1950s from an amalgamation of rhythm and blues and country music and characterised by a heavy beat and simple repeated melodies; a style of music characterised by a basic drum-beat, generally 4/4 riffs, based on (usually electric) guitar, drums and vocals (generally with bass guitar).

role model a person who provides a good example; for example, gender role models are thought to be particularly important for growing children.

Romanticism a movement in the arts, music and literature which originated in the late 18th century emphasising inspiration, subjectivity and the primacy of the individual; a style which describes the beauty of nature and emphasises the importance of human emotions.

sanction a threatened penalty for disobeying a law or rule; measures taken by a state to force another to conform to an international agreement; to impose a penalty on an offender.

satire the use of humour, irony, exaggeration or ridicule to expose and criticise stupidity or vice; a literary technique of writing or art which principally ridicules its subject often as an intended means of provoking or preventing change; a way of criticising people or ideas in a humorous way.

science fiction fiction based on imagined future worlds portraying scientific or technological changes, especially about space travel or other worlds.

Scottish Parliament body based in Edinburgh, to which the UK Parliament has devolved a range of legislative and executive powers.

SDLP (Social Democratic and Labour Party) a moderate political party in Northern Ireland mainly supported by the Roman Catholic and nationalist communities; in recent years it has been overshadowed by the emergence of Sinn Fein as the main channel of opposition to the Protestant and unionist political parties.

secular the opposite of religious.

self-censorship the exercising of control over what one reads, views, says or does, especially to avoid reprisal or offence; control of what you say or do in order to avoid annoying or offending others, but without being told officially that such control is necessary.

self-image how a person sees or identifies her or himself, e.g. English or Scottish, male or female, gay or straight, young or old, healthy or sick. Self-image may sometimes be broadly the same as the way an individual's friends or work colleagues perceive them, though psychological and other problems may arise if a significant gap arises between the two.

sexism discrimination, even hatred, towards people based on their sex rather than their personal qualities/achievements or other individual merits; it can be manifested as the belief that one gender or sex is inferior to or more valuable than the other.

Short money public funds paid to opposition MPs at Westminster to allow them to employ researchers to offset the advantages of the government party which has access to the work of civil servants; so called because Edward Short was Leader of the House of Commons when the scheme was introduced in 1974. The sums paid in 2007/8 (based on votes gained at the 2005 general election) included £4.5 million to the Conservatives and £1.6 million to the Liberal Democrats.

Sinn Fein political party favouring a united Ireland and supported by Irish nationalists and Roman Catholics in both Eire and Ulster; this party is now the largest nationalist party in the Northern Ireland Assembly and leads the power sharing administration with the Democratic Unionist Party, following the Good Friday Agreement of 1998. There were five Sinn Fein MPs elected to Westminster in 2005; they do not take their seats because they were unwilling to take an Oath of Allegiance to HM The Queen.

skyscraper a very tall modern building of many stories or floors.

soap opera a television or radio drama serial dealing with daily events in the lives of the same group of characters; so named because such serials were originally sponsored by US soap manufacturers in the 1930s; they concern the lives of melodramatic characters, which are often filled with strong emotions, highly dramatic situations and suspense.

social contract the general idea that individuals give up some of their freedom or their assumed 'natural state' so that a community or nation can maintain order. This in turn benefits all citizens.

Social Democratic and Labour Party see **SDLP**.

social engineering interventions, often by government, to seek to change how people behave within society, e.g. by developing education programmes to create a more equal society so far as opportunities are concerned.

social exclusion the alienation or disenfranchisement of certain people within a society, often connected to a person's social class, educational status and living standards and how the opportunities open to an individual may be limited. The disabled, men and women, those from ethnic minorities and the elderly from all races are liable to be affected

social inclusion the coordinated response to the very complex system of problems that are known as social exclusion.

social mobility the degree to which an individual's, family's or group's social status can change through a system of social hierarchy or stratification. Subsequently, it is also the degree to which that individual's or group's descendants move up and down the class system. Social mobility is thought to be much lower in the UK than in other countries.

social reaction theory see **labelling theory**.

social stratification the hierarchical arrangement of social classes or castes within a society.

socialisation, primary the process whereby people learn usually within their early years and mainly within the family the attitudes, values and actions appropriate to individuals as members of a particular culture.

socialisation, secondary the process of learning what is appropriate behaviour as a member of a smaller group within the larger society (e.g. at school, at university, in a sports club, at work). It is usually associated with teenagers and adults, and involves smaller changes than those occurring in primary socialisation, e.g. entering a new profession, relocating to a new environment or society.

society a particular community of people; a long-standing group of people sharing cultural aspects such as language, dress, norms of behaviour and artistic forms; the people of one's country or community taken as a whole; a large group of people who live together in an organised way, making decisions about how to do things and sharing the work that needs to be done; all the people in a country, or in several similar countries, can be referred to as a society.

solicitor a member of the legal profession qualified to deal with conveyancing, draw up wills, advise clients, prepare cases and instruct barristers and represent clients in lower courts.

solidarity see **class solidarity**.

spin a favourable bias or slant given to a news story, to make ideas, events etc. seem better than they really are, especially in politics.

sponsor a person or organisation that pays for or contributes to the costs of sporting, broadcast or artistic events in return for advertising.

stability of society the state that occurs when social processes work in accordance with the laws and underlying cultural values of a society.

standard of living refers to the quality and quantity of goods and services available to people, and the way these goods and services are distributed within a population. It expresses the quality of life for individuals in monetary terms, and may be calculated by dividing the national income for any period by the population; in terms of inequality in the UK many people will have an income (purchasing power) far above the average, while others have an income substantially below the average.

state funding (of political parties) the proposal that political parties should be funded by the state to avoid the many controversies involving funding from trade unions, companies, private organisations and overseas bodies; those in favour of state funding believe democracy cannot be taken for granted or left to the motives of those donors who may give with some self-interested purpose in mind.

status relative social or professional standing; the official classification given to a person determining their rights or responsibilities; position or rank, especially in a social group; a person's position or standing relative to that of others.

statute a written law passed by a legislative body; a rule of an organisation or institution; a law or decree made by a sovereign.

statutory powers powers granted, required or enacted by statute.

stem cells cells found in all multi-cellular organisms which can renew themselves through mitotic cell division and can differentiate into a range of specialised cell types. The two broad types of mammalian stem cells are embryonic stem cells and adult stem cells that are found in adult tissues. In a developing embryo, stem cells can differentiate into all of the specialised embryonic tissues. In adult organisms, stem cells and progenitor cells act as a repair system for the body, replenishing specialised cells, but also maintain the normal turnover of regenerative organs, such as blood, skin or intestinal tissues.

stipendiary receiving a stipend (a fixed regular sum paid as a salary); working for pay rather than voluntarily.

sub-culture a group of people with a culture involving distinctively different values which differentiate them from the larger, more general society to which they belong. See also **youth culture**.

summary a judicial process conducted without the customary legal formalities; a conviction made by a judge or magistrate without a jury.

summary offence an offence within the scope of a summary court.

supply an ability and willingness to supply goods and services; prices usually rise if demand exceeds supply and fall if supply exceeds demand. See also **demand**.

surveillance society term used by the Information Commissioner to refer to the way in which the lives and personal details of individuals are monitored and arguably involve unwarranted intrusion into personal liberty and privacy, e.g. through CCTV images in most town centres, credit and debit card transactions, use of identity cards, supermarket loyalty cards and mobile phone records.

survey a general view, examination or description; an investigation of the opinion or experience of a group of people based on a series of questions.

symbol a thing that represents or stands for something else; a material object representing something abstract.

Symbolism the use of symbols to represent ideas or qualities; an artistic style originating in the late 19th century using symbolic images and indirect suggestions to express mystical ideas, emotions and states of mind.

tactical voting a process that occurs in single member constituencies using the first part the post electoral system (as in UK general elections); it involves individual voters deciding which candidate or party has the best chance of defeating the candidate or party they like least; typically voters switch from candidates likely to come third or fourth to those who are likely to come first or second.

tag(ging) an electronic device attached to someone or something for monitoring purposes.

talent natural aptitude or skill.

tariff a standard scale of sentences and damages for crimes and injuries of different severity.

taxation, direct a sum paid directly to the government by individuals on whom it is imposed; direct taxes include income tax, council tax and inheritance tax.

taxation, indirect (or **'collected' tax**) a sum collected by intermediaries (i.e. indirectly) who pay the proceeds to the government; it is not collected directly by the government or paid directly to them by the individual. Indirect taxes include value added tax (VAT) or airport departure tax.

technology the application of scientific knowledge for practical purposes; machinery and equipment based on scientific knowledge.

telecommunications the sending and receiving of messages over a distance using cable, telegraph, telephone or broadcasting; the branch of technology concerned with this type of communication; the science and technology of communication at a distance, especially the electronic transmission of signals.

terrorism the use of terror (extreme fear) to intimidate people; the deliberate commission of an act of violence to create an emotional response from the victim in the furtherance of a political or social agenda; violence against civilians to achieve military or political objectives; a psychological strategy of war for gaining political or religious ends by deliberately creating a climate of fear among the population of a state.

terrorist a person who uses violence and intimidation in pursuit of political aims in an attempt to coerce a more powerful opponent, such as a government.

theft the action or crime of dishonestly taking and keeping something which belongs to someone else.

theory (scientific) an explanation of a phenomenon or phenomena which has been tested by experiment. The experiment may confirm that the explanation is still a good one, or it may set out to disprove (falsify) the explanation. The word 'theory' is sometimes used in a non-scientific context to imply that an explanation has little worth (e.g. 'It's only a theory!') but in science a theory is our best explanation possible, until the theory is disproved. See also **hypothesis (scientific)**.

torture the action or practice of deliberately inflicting severe pain (whether physical or mental) as a punishment or as a forcible means of persuasion or simply to cause suffering.

totalitarian of or relating to a centralised and dictatorial system of government which requires complete subservience to the state; a system of government where the people have virtually no authority and the state wields absolute control over every aspect of life in the country, socially, financially and politically.

trend a general direction in which something is changing or developing; a fashion.

tribunal a special court or group of people established by the government to examine legal problems and settle certain kinds of dispute; a court of justice.

Turner prize an annual prize presented to a British visual artist under 50, named after the painter J.M.W. Turner. It is organised by the Tate Gallery and staged at Tate Britain. Since its beginnings in 1984 it has become the United Kingdom's most publicised art award, being associated with conceptual art, although it represents all media and painters have also won the prize. There have

been different sponsors, including Channel 4 television and Gordon's gin. It is a controversial event, mainly for its exhibits.

twocing taking without owner's consent; slang police term for stealing a car.

UKIP United Kingdom Independence Party, which achieved its greatest success in the 2004 elections for the European Parliament when it won 12 seats (same as the Liberal Democrats); it opposes the UK's EU membership. The party has no MPs and has had trouble with some of its MEPs, e.g. Ashley Mote went to prison for benefit fraud, Godfrey Bloom outraged public opinion when he said no self-respecting small businessman with a brain in the right place would ever employ a lady of child-bearing age.

Ulster Unionist Party once the foremost Protestant political party in Northern Ireland until it was overtaken by the Democratic Unionist Party. In 2005 just one Ulster Unionist MP was elected compared to nine for the DUP.

UN see **United Nations**.

UN Security Council a body which exists to respond to urgent situations; there are five permanent members including the UK all of which can veto (block) a proposal and also ten other countries which are elected to serve on the council for a specified period.

unemployment, frictional occurs when a worker moves from one job to another. While s/he searches for a job s/he is experiencing frictional unemployment.

unemployment, seasonal occurs when an occupation is not in demand at certain seasons.

unemployment, structural caused by a mismatch between the location of jobs and the location of job-seekers; 'location' may be geographical, or in terms of skills. The mismatch arises because the unemployed are unwilling or unable to change geography or skills.

United Nations (UN) worldwide alliance of 192 countries based in New York; often finds it difficult to act decisively because of disagreements between member countries; the UN has many agencies with humanitarian and development objectives including peace-keeping.

universal(istic) of, affecting or done by all people or things in the world or in a particular group.

urban of or relating to a town or city; characteristic of city life.

utilitarianism a form of moral reasoning that judges an act on whether it produces the greatest happiness for the greatest number. See also consequentialism.

utopia an imagined perfect place or state of things; a perfect society in which everyone works well with each other and is happy; 'utopian' means ideal but often impractical. See also **dystopia**.

values principles, beliefs or standards that are considered subjective and not universal and vary across people and cultures. Types of values include ethical or moral values, political, religious values, social values and aesthetic values. Personal values evolve from interaction with the external world, from influences such as culture, religion and political party, and may change over time, though values developed early in life may be resistant to change.

victim a person harmed, injured or killed as a result of a crime or accident; an aggrieved or disadvantaged party in a crime.

victims' rights the Victims' Code of Practice came into force in 2006, and sets out the minimum standards of information and support that victims of crime can expect to receive from each of the criminal justice agencies, including the police, CPS and Her Majesty's Court Service. It gives a right to information about their crime with specified timescales, including the right to be notified of any arrests and court cases. It also requires a dedicated family liaison police officer to be assigned to bereaved relatives; clear information from the Criminal Injuries Compensation Authority on eligibility for compensation under the scheme; all victims to be told about Victim Support and referred to them, if appropriate; and an enhanced service for vulnerable or intimidated victims.

watershed the time (usually 9 pm) after which programmes 'of a more adult nature' that are regarded as unsuitable for children may be broadcast on television.

welfare state based on Lord Beveridge's proposals, the welfare state sought to eliminate the 'giant evils' of poverty, ignorance, idleness, disease and squalor by drastically improving levels/standards of pensions and social security payments, education, full employment, health and housing.

Welsh Assembly assembly based in Cardiff to which the UK Parliament has devolved a range of legislative and executive powers.

white-collar crime crime associated with people who work in an office or other professional environment; crime committed by a person of respectability and high social status in the course of his or her occupation. The opportunity for fraud, bribery, insider trading, embezzlement, computer crime and forgery is more available to white-collar employees than manual workers. See also **blue-collar crime**.

working-class crime see **blue-collar crime**.

youth culture a youth-based sub-culture with distinctive styles, behaviours and interests; members of this sub-culture often signal their membership by making distinctive and symbolic tangible choices, e.g. in clothes, hairstyles and footwear. They will probably have shared interests, dialects and slang; music genres, meeting places and values can also be important factors. Youth sub-cultures offer participants an identity separate from that ascribed by formally recognised institutions such as family, work, home and school. See also **sub-culture**.

Answers

Multiple choice questions, unit 1, pages 49–54

1. D	7. D	13. A	19. C
2. B	8. B	14. C	20. D
3. A	9. B	15. A	21. (a) A, (b) C
4. C	10. C	16. B	22. D
5. A	11. C	17. A	
6. D	12. C	18. (a) B, (b) B	

Multiple choice questions, unit 2, pages 101–5

1. D	7. C	13. D	19. B
2. B	8. D	14. A	20. D
3. C	9. B	15. B	21. B
4. A	10. B	16. C	22. C
5. C	11. A	17. D	23. B
6. B	12. A	18. C	

Data response practice question, unit 1, pages 122–3

Mark scheme: key points

(a) Such points as
- this would be a way of keeping in touch with parents or grandparents
- they could make contact in an emergency
- it provides a way for the family to find them if they 'disappear'

(b) Such points as
- might run up large bills
- might cause health problems in later life
- youngsters not mature enough – may not be old enough to tie shoe laces

(c) Such points as
- big firms direct mailing youngsters or showing television adverts when they are viewing will cause much 'pester power'
- poor parents may not be able to afford such phones, so the company's marketing may cause conflict in the home between child and parent
- better off parents could afford phones but may feel that to succumb to marketing pressure could lead to health issues for their child later in life

(d) Such points as
- in a democracy, politicians need to respond to voter concerns
- so far as health is concerned, prevention can be better than cure, so if there is doubt a minister is right to express a view
- if concerned parents are pressing for a marketing ban (as on cigarettes) this has a better chance of being achieved if the mind of the minister is engaged on the issue

(e) (i) Argument from analogy
    (ii) Such points as
- the addiction parallel is a good one
- so the analogy 'works' as a form of reasoning in this instance
- often analogies do not work so well because the parallel is less apposite

Data response practice question, unit 2, pages 124–5

Mark scheme: key points

(a) The **only** acceptable extract is: Dr John Dunford warned yesterday.

(b) Because Dr Dunford is said to be a former headteacher and therefore an expert on matters concerning schools and children

(c) Such factors as
- the decline of marriage
- the rise of divorce
- an increase in cohabitation (i.e. often less permanent relationships)
- many more single parents (poor, lack of time, being pressured to go to work)

(d) Allow any genuinely moral judgements – such factors as
- telling the truth
- behaving honestly
- showing concern for others

(e) (i) Deductive argument
   (ii) Such points as
   - for a deductive argument, if the premises (a previous statement from which another is inferred) are true it would be impossible for the conclusion to be false
   - but an inductive argument based on observations will provide reasons for supporting the *probable* truth of a conclusion

(f) The answer should consider such questions as
- what is the balance between fact and opinion?
- are there too many opinions, i.e. would any case be simply an opinionated statement?
- how much difference does it make if the opinions given are (in some cases) those of an expert authority?
- some facts are stated in the passage: how relevant to the topic are these facts?

Extended writing practice question, page 137

Mark scheme

AO1 (relevant knowledge and understanding) 8 marks
Identification of factors
Award 1 mark for each point, up to the maximum of 8 marks, such as:

1. the Abortion Act gave women legal control over their own fertility
2. divorce reform created many more single parent families, with children often placed with mothers who were therefore disadvantaged in employment and income terms
3. equal pay acts were an attempt to establish greater equality but there are still significant differences between potential earnings of men and women
4. the Sex Discrimination Act made it illegal to discriminate on grounds of gender
5. the influence of EU employment legislation
6. the Commission for Equality and Human Rights brings together work of various equality commissions
7. laws have to be implemented and women (especially the low paid) are rarely in a position to protect their own interests

8. women as carers are often unable to take employment that matches their ability or qualifications because of the need to look after children or aged parents

9. the costs of child care are high and often make employment less attractive in spite of legislation

10. the failure of the Child Support Agency to provide mothers with adequate resources

11. changes in taxation law have attempted to improve the position of women

Note that references to contraception are not strictly relevant to 'government attempts' but may be linked to employment laws.

AO2 (marshal evidence and draw conclusions) 8 marks
Award up to 3 marks for relevant arguments within each of the following areas up to an overall maximum of 8 marks.

Understanding and evaluation of the meaning of gender equality E.g.:
- refers both to employment and social circumstances
- finance is a key to making aspects of equality real for the individual
- changed social attitudes have influenced government action
- non-government/legislative influences have been more significant (increased education opportunities; changing attitudes to sex and sexuality; contraception; changed attitudes to marriage etc.)

Arguments to suggest government efforts have been successful E.g.:
- more women work and experience longer periods of education than before
- increasing number of women in senior positions in employment
- more women able to leave unsuccessful marriages and support themselves
- lack of recent legislation

Arguments to suggest government efforts have been unsuccessful E.g.:
- there are still significant pay differentials
- single mothers are generally amongst the poorer sections of population
- most 'top jobs' are still held by men
- increased educational opportunities are masked because more women follow 'softer' academic routes than men

Published by:
Pearson Education Limited
Edinburgh Gate
Harlow
Essex CM20 2JE

First published 2008
10 9 8 7 6
ISBN: 978-1-8469-0320-5

The publisher would like to thank the following for their kind
permission to reproduce their photographs:

Alamy Images: Andrew Paterson 83; Arco Images GmbH 75;
Classic Stock 55; Duncan Hale-Sutton 67; Mark Sykes 91;
Photo Researchers 9; Red Green Blue New Media Ltd Gonta 25;
Corbis: Image Source 17; **Mary Evans Picture Library:** 41

All other images © Pearson Education

Picture Research by: Alison Prior
Page make-up and illustrations by: Redmoor Design,
Tavistock, Devon

We are grateful to the following for their permission to reproduce
copyright material: Page 49, The *New Scientist* for their article on
mobile phone alarms; page 122 The New York times for their article
'Concern in Europe on Cellphone Ads for Children' The New York
Times, 08/03/08 © 2008 The New York Times. All rights reserved.
Used by permission and protected by the Copyright Laws of the
United States. The printing, copying, redistribution or retransmission
of the Material without express written permission is prohibited.

Every effort has been made to trace the copyright holders and we
apologise in advance for any unintentional omissions. We would
be pleased to insert the appropriate acknowledgement in any
subsequent edition of this publication.

Printed in Malaysia (CTP-VVP)